MW01088130

# PRAISE FOR *LOVE, POLITICS, AND OTHER SCARY THINGS*

"This is the perfect gift for any woman (or man) disappointed by the defeat of Kamala Harris. Susan Platt has written a book that is an enjoyable read—even the sad parts—based on her own experiences in politics with her late husband Ron. Win or lose, Susan shows us there's always something to be gained by getting off the bench and into the game. This book will inspire you to try out for the team, whatever your party and ideology."

**PROFESSOR LARRY SABATO**
THE CENTER FOR POLITICS AT THE UNIVERSITY OF VIRGINIA

"Susan and Ron never shied away from doing what they believed in—even if it was scary. Her experience, influence, and heart are everywhere evident in this book, as is Ron's permeating influence. Whether she's discussing her marriage with Ron, or the highs and lows of political life, Susan's voice is inspiring, and her message is one to be cherished."

**US SENATOR MARK R. WARNER (VA)**

"I have known and admired Susan Platt for over thirty years, first as a remarkable political consultant, then as a colleague working to support more women to run for elective office—Susan herself becoming a candidate for Lt. Governor in 2017—and finally as a friend. I never dreamed she was a writer as well *Love, Politics and Other Scary Things* is wonderful. It is fresh and inspiring; reading it will encourage you to try scary things that don't kill you."

**THE HONORABLE MARY SUE TERRY**
FORMER ATTORNEY GENERAL OF VIRGINIA AND
FIRST WOMAN TO HOLD STATEWIDE OFFICE IN VIRGINIA

"Susan Platt's memoir is a beautiful and poignant retrospective on her career in the top echelon of DC politics, her journey navigating love and loss, and the path, sometimes crooked and difficult, to finding her voice and purpose. But as much as it chronicles her life up to this point, it also looks toward the future with courage and hope and compels us to do the same. Susan's is a life story from which anyone can draw inspiration and strength."

US SENATOR TIM KAINE (VA)

"Susan's willingness to share her life story in such an honest way—including facing challenges like illness, loss, and grief —will be an inspiration for readers. This book is a tribute to strong women, and I hope it encourages more women to run for office themselves."

US SENATOR AMY KLOBUCHAR (MN)

LOVE,
POLITICS,
AND OTHER
SCARY THINGS

a memoir

# LOVE, POLITICS, AND OTHER SCARY THINGS

## Susan Smocer Platt

BOLD
STORY
PRESS

CHEVY CHASE, MD

Bold Story Press, Chevy Chase, MD 20815
www.boldstorypress.com

First edition: December 2024
Library of Congress Control Number: 2024923687
ISBN: 978-1-954805-79-8 (hardcover)
ISBN: 978-1-954805-81-1 (paperback)
ISBN: 978-1-954805-80-4 (e-book)

Cover and interior design by KP Books
Printed in the United States of America
10  9  8  7  6  5  4  3  2  1

To my husband, Ron,
who was my inspiration in love, life, and purpose.
Your twinkling lights inspire me to forge on
with you by my side, if only in spirit.

*Being deeply loved by someone gives you strength,*
*while loving someone deeply gives you courage.*

LAO TZU

# CONTENTS

CONTENTS

## PART THREE: THE LOSS

# PROLOGUE

I awoke with a jolt. I had been dreaming that I was cradling Ron under my right arm and holding his left hand in mine. In the dream, he opened his eyes, looked into mine, and told me he was going to be all right. I remember thinking something was wrong. At this point, Ron was not conscious. The doctors told me the MRI showed his brain activity was diminished from lack of oxygen due to pneumonia and sepsis. He was dying. When I opened my eyes, I was lying on a hospital cot in the ICU, holding Ron, touching as much of his body as I could with mine. Not one inch separated us. It was just like my dream. I told the nurses I wanted to lie next to him all night, so they rolled a bed in from an empty room. They added another mattress on top so both beds would be even, and they lifted the headboard halfway on my side to be level with Ron's. The lights were out in the room and dimmed in the ICU hallway. A curtain surrounded the bed, and through the top I could see low lighting in the hall, but I had enough light to read the clock high on the wall; it was 1:30 a.m. When I turned and looked at Ron, he didn't appear to be struggling or in pain. There were no sounds; everything that could beep had been removed from him. I was trying to shake the unsettling feeling I had from the dream, and

I just lay there, squeezing his hand and holding on to him as if I could keep him with me always.

Suddenly, I saw something out of the corner of my eye. Something was moving—a cluster of small beams of twinkling lights, like Tinker Bell fairy lights—dancing over Ron's lap. I just stared at them, not understanding what I was seeing. I looked all around and saw there was no other light in the room and nowhere they could be coming from. I knew I was not asleep; it was not my imagination: the lights were there. I have no idea how long I watched those lights; I was mesmerized as I watched the swirling mass of tiny white lights dance. For that moment in time, nothing else mattered but watching those lights. It is hard for me to describe the feelings I had, but I remember I was calm and at peace. It was magical. It was real. It was spiritual. It was love. I don't know and may never know what the lights meant. They could have been Ron's energy trying to connect with me and tell me goodbye. Maybe it was God. But I knew instinctively that I was loved and at that moment I was not alone.

A friend later told me I was hallucinating—that it's something that happens during stressful times. A priest told me not to tell anyone, as others might think me strange, or they might be jealous that this spiritual event happened to me. Another young priest had a different reaction. Over a lunch that included several glasses of wine, I told him my story about the dancing lights. His reaction was one I had hoped to hear from the first priest. He told me how blessed I had been to have had such a wonderful marriage and to experience the mystery of the dancing lights. He suggested I didn't need an explanation for them, and I've come to believe it really didn't matter. What I do know is that it was a special communication Ron and I shared and one that would influence the rest of my life.

What do you do when the love of your life is gone—when you have lived for forty-three years with the ultimate partner for you? Who are you now? How do you go on and navigate your life again, alone? Did I even want to? The questions continue while I search for those answers.

But those dancing lights give me the strength to keep living while trying to work through the grief and find joy and fulfillment in my life again.

# PART ONE

# BEFORE

# 1

## Fried Okra and Haluski or Chicken Fried Steak and Hoagies?

When I was young, I pushed myself to experience all I could. What did I have to lose? I believed I would certainly die from illness by the age of forty, as my mother had, so I lived as though I had an early expiration date. I found myself asking these questions about what I would do in my life. Would I be bold, or would I be cautious? Would I test my limits, or would I stay in my comfort zone? Would I be a success or a failure? Would my anxiety keep me from living a life overflowing with love, adventure, and purpose? But I got lucky when I met the man who became my true love and found what I was searching for in love and politics.

How did a girl from the gritty, smoky, industrial mid-Atlantic city of Pittsburgh, Pennsylvania, meet and fall in love with a cowboy from the small rural town of Ada, Oklahoma? When they say opposites attract, that could not have been truer about us. I had never tasted okra or chicken fried steak, and Ron had never heard of hoagies or *haluski*. He had earned two college degrees while married with children, and I hadn't even finished my last year of undergrad. Ron knew he wanted a career in politics; I was unfocused, directionless, and always in a hurry. But a young man from rural Oklahoma and an even younger woman from a steel town in Pennsylvania would find they had a lot in common. As the cliché says, we were two imperfect people who made a perfect match. We were opposites in many ways, but we would complement each other. We would find in each other traits that we felt we might lack individually. We were becoming true partners in life and would find our purpose as partners in Washington, DC. Like a lot of other couples who were drawn to political life, we were always dealing with one crisis or another. We were always managing political crises while trying to maintain a solid, loving, and nurturing home life.

When Ron landed at National Airport in Washington, DC, in the 1960s, he knew he was in the right place. He often said he felt deep inside that this was where he would find his home, the place he was meant to be, and he never looked back. He had too much he wanted to do, and if you wanted a career in politics, DC was the place to be. Once he moved there, he never looked back.

Before we were married, I had never been to Oklahoma. I imagined it was filled with cowboys and oil wells. Ron was sometimes embarrassed to admit he was from Oklahoma and would say he was from Texas instead (at the time, Texas was politically a more important state). Not until after Ron died did I learn from another Oklahoman that they too rarely admitted they were from Oklahoma. This was something I never understood. I would correct him when he would say he was from Texas, and he would say, "Well, politically I am from Texas," because it was where he taught American government and became involved in running political campaigns. He felt inferior about getting his degrees from the University of Oklahoma when many of his colleagues had attended Ivy League schools.

Ron was born in 1941 to parents who barely received a high school education. Ron's father, Hook, never graduated high school, was a carpenter, and then owned a service station with a partner. He could fix anything that needed fixing, a skill his son never learned. Hook at times could be a bit of a partier and a flirt, so at the instigation of Ron's mother, Maggie, his parents agreed that she would oversee Ronnie's upbringing. Maggie was a bookkeeper at the local drug store. During the 1940s and 1950s, women rarely worked full time outside the home, particularly when they had children. Ron's cherished maternal grandmother, Mama Barker, was there to chip in with early child-rearing.

Maggie's temperament leaned toward cold remoteness. I have often thought that if times had been different, Maggie would have chosen a career over motherhood. Hook and Maggie would only have one child. Ron's birth was difficult, and Maggie never let him forget it. They said they wanted their child to have better opportunities than they did and were determined their child would have a college degree. They believed they could save enough money to give that opportunity to only one child.

Ron was an anxious and introverted child, and those traits continued into adulthood. He was quick to please others, and he hated conflict. He used to say he really didn't know why, but at some point, I think he figured it out. In the last few years of his life, he relayed a story to me of a childhood incident with his mother that he believed made him anxious and left an indelible scar on him and their relationship.

All children argue with their parents, and Ron was no different; he was hardheaded and incredibly smart. One afternoon, while Ron was arguing with his mother, she reached a breaking point. She grabbed him and held him so tightly against herself he could not breathe. She eventually came to her senses and released him; she cried and said how sorry she was and begged him to forgive her. While he forgave her lapse of judgment, the episode affected him in ways he would never forget. I always wondered why their relationship was not close and loving but just chalked it up to her remote personality. After he told me what had happened, I understood his attitude.

Oklahoma was cowboy boots country, and Ron wore them from the time he could walk. He loved ham hocks and beans, fried okra, and sausage gravy. He had a horse from the time he was a young boy. He had a motorcycle, fast cars, and girls. He loved dogs and had a black-and-white cocker spaniel named Spot, who was stolen from his yard, leaving him heartbroken. Although shy, he was handsome and popular with a quick wit, and he was a favorite among the girls. In his elementary school years, his favorite thing to do was read *The Hardy Boys* books for hours. Ronnie was dyslexic and taught himself to read, as he described to me, by taking snapshots of paragraphs. I never could figure out how he did it, but he read faster than anyone I ever met, and he understood it all. Friday night football games were important in the small town, but unfortunately for him, his slight build kept him on the bench, while his older cousin coached the team that held several statewide championships.

Churchgoing was important in the rural south, and Ron's family became members of the Pentecost Holiness Church. Ron not only attended church with his parents but was also enrolled in Sunday school. He was also a fan of the "the-A-ter," as it was pronounced, and rock and roll, and Elvis. According to the Sunday school teacher, this was sinful behavior. She brought Ron to the front of the class, where he was shamed as a sinner.

Ron went home and told his parents what she had done and how it made him feel and insisted he would never go back to that church or Sunday school. As Ron told the story, and added with a smirk, shortly after that, the church burned down. Although he always claimed he had nothing to do with it, he would add a sly hee-haw whenever he told the story. So much for organized religion. This proved to be a pivotal moment in young Ronnie's life. I believe the humiliating experience of being shamed ignited a spark in him that led him toward his interest in politics and a lifetime of fighting against hate, injustice, and discrimination.

Ron's childhood friend Ted Granger remembers that Ron was usually ahead of cultural waves. He was the first one in Ada to play Elvis records and enjoy the music that inspired it, and the first in Ada to own a Vespa motorcycle. He loved to drag race on Main Street. Ted also noted that Ronnie and his first wife, Jeanne, were the only ones in their high school class who didn't have to get married! And Ron was the first to discover a young politician from Massachusetts, Congressman John F. Kennedy, whose political philosophy would be one of the reasons Ron got his master's degree and studied for a PhD in political science, taught college-level American government, and ultimately found his way to Washington, DC.

Thirteen years after Ron was born, I entered the world in Pittsburgh, Pennsylvania, and for my first four years, my parents and I lived in the small suburb of Turtle Creek.

My mother, Julia Helen Gaslevic, was valedictorian of her high school class and became the first woman auditor for the Navy in Pittsburgh. My father, Tony, had just returned from a stint in the Navy as a radarman. At the encouragement of my mother, he took his GED and applied to attend Carnegie Technical Institute, majoring in engineering. My father loved to take things apart and put them back better. He became a senior engineer at Westinghouse, designing parts for nuclear reactors for the Navy, where he was awarded the most patents ever at the Bettis location. Among his many accomplishments, Dad loved to dance, and he had a side job teaching dance at Arthur Murray Dance Studio. Dad was one of twelve children, and the only one of his siblings to attend college.

We lived on the top floor of a two-story duplex, where my mother's mother, sister, and brother-in-law lived on the main level. My room had a beautiful evening sky with stars painted on the ceiling. I remember my aunt Kate giving me a hula-hoop and telling me how to use it. I remember playing in the backyard, in a white frilly dress, with our black-and-white dog, Ditto, and picking flowers and placing them in my grandmother's lap. One sunny afternoon she was sitting outside with me while I picked flowers, and I tried to wake her, but she wouldn't open her eyes. I remember the sun shining and my grandmother smiling, and I know she was happy.

With both parents working good jobs, we moved out of the duplex to our own home in a more affluent community, where life held a lot of promise for my parents and me. Unfortunately, that promise didn't last long, as my mother was diagnosed with an aggressive form of breast cancer. Several years of hospitals and nannies followed. I had birthday parties. I went to school with Heidi, my neighbor and best friend throughout my life. I played kickball in the alley behind our house, and Dad made a swing for me that hung from our apple tree. I had a nanny from Wales, Mae, who would have tea and cookies ready for me when I got home from school. I also had my precious black poodle, Holly, to cuddle.

My mother spent a lot of time in hospitals in Pittsburgh and New York City. The few times she was home, she spent most of her time in bed. I remember opening the door to the bathroom once and seeing her bald head; she quickly closed the door before I could ask any questions. Shortly after, she came out wearing a perfectly styled wig. Back in the 1960s, cancer and the effects of chemo were not openly discussed, especially with a young girl. I have very few memories of her, but I do recall a time when she said she wanted to talk to me. She called me in from playing outside and asked me to sit on the bed next to her, and I remember her using the words "the birds and the bees." I had no idea what she was talking about. As I think back on it, it must have been something she really wanted to be the one to tell me because I was too young to understand what she was explaining. I knew my life was different from that of my other friends whose mothers were home with them, but I just went along and did most things any young girl would do.

One day in early January, the school principal took me out of class saying my dad wanted to see me at home. Mae took me home, where Dad brought me into his bedroom and on his knees. Holding my arms, he said, "Susan, God has taken Mommy to heaven." I didn't understand what death really meant, but I knew that Dad was trying to hold back his heartbreak and was failing. I had never seen my father so vulnerable, and that frightened me, so I cried too. The funeral is mostly a rainy blur. I found myself standing close to my father, watching him, not letting him out of my sight. I remember attending the funeral Mass at St. Bernard's

Catholic Church. I remember crying and my father putting his hand on my shoulder and telling me quietly to be strong and not to cry, so I stopped. For years after, every time I said the words *my mother*, my voice quivered.

My father didn't take me to the burial at the gravesite, so I just sat waiting for him to return home for the gathering of family and friends after. I have snapshots of memory from that afternoon: my uncle pointed out we had caviar—that was a first; it had to be an incredibly special occasion to have caviar. Someone asked for my mother's chocolate cake recipe. But that is all I remember. I don't even know how I felt; I was just watching the day unfold.

Early that spring, I suspect my father thought it was time for us to take a few days away, and the two of us went to Washington, DC, to see the cherry blossoms. I do not know the reason he picked this time or place, but I remember being extremely excited to go on this trip with him. Just the two of us. It was just us now, and we were beginning to settle in with the new reality. We toured all the monuments and the White House and drove around the Tidal Basin, enjoying the cherry blossoms in full bloom. I remember looking out the window of the taxi several times and seeing my mother walking on the sidewalk and pointing her out to him. He would just look at me and hug me and say that was someone who looked like her. I remember thinking how strange that was and knowing it was not possible, but I wanted to believe it. I have often wondered about that trip and whether it led to my spending my life and career in Washington.

Several months after my mother's death, my poodle, Holly, was run over by a car. I was just beginning to understand the permanence of death. I was heartbroken as I petted her still body on a blanket in a cardboard box. My dad just let me wail and patiently waited until I realized there was nothing to do except grieve the loss. Two losses separated by such a few months felt like more than I could manage, but soon there would be another dog, Ivy, to love.

Life would continue as normally as it could. I loved to run and play sports outside but was always a little shy. I was never one to play with baby dolls; Barbie was more my speed. Being a mother and having a child of my own was never something I gave much thought to. My father went to work every day, and Heidi and I would walk to school—Heidi with her cello and me with my snare drum and cymbal.

At about this time, a seemingly insignificant event would leave an indelible mark on my personality. One day in gym class at school while trying to kick a ball during a game, I tripped, fell, and broke my arm. I remember thinking it was not very painful, and it seemed cool to have a cast on my arm. Well, Mae would have none of it. She said, "It's not as if your father doesn't have enough to worry about—now you've gone and broken your arm!" This was such an incredible "aha" moment for me. I remember something like a light bulb going off in my brain. Like Ron's shaming at Sunday school, this event opened my eyes to empathy, care about others, and being considerate. Although I was quite young, I saw that I had been more consumed with myself than others; this is the moment that changed.

My father remarried eighteen months later, to Barbara, the daughter of good friends, and they would soon grow their—our—family with my brother, Michael and sister, Jessica.

After I graduated from high school in January of 1973, my father asked me if I wanted to go to college. Instead, I got an apartment with two other girls and began working two jobs, one during the day and the other in the evening. I took the bus to downtown Pittsburgh for my salesclerk job in the morning, then rode the bus back to the suburbs for the evening job as receptionist at a karate studio. At first, I felt like I was having the time of my life. Then, my body run down from constant work, I got a serious case of strep throat and could not work. My father knew the time had come again to ask me about going to college, only this time I agreed. Being on my own and responsible for all my bills was harder than I anticipated.

I started my first semester at the University of Pittsburgh, Johnstown campus, in June of 1973. Since I decided so late that I wanted to go to college, I needed to begin in the summer session and make all Bs to attend the fall semester, and that was after my stepmother's father who was on the board asked for a favor. I decided I wanted to major in sociology, so I began with several of those courses.

My first day on campus, I spotted Tony, who would be my first cowboy boyfriend, at a welcome softball game. At first sight I was smitten. Tony was about the handsomest boy I had ever seen, had the cutest smile with twinkling mischievous eyes, wore blue jeans and cowboy boots, and drove the sexiest car of that time, a blue Datsun 240Z. Lucky for me, I caught his eye as well. When I think back on that time, I still see him in my mind's eye walking in a blizzard across campus, with his cowboy boots and hat and leather book bag. He walked with such purpose, attitude, and charisma. Before long we were dating each other exclusively. It was the seventies with sex, drugs, and rock and roll and rebelling against authority, and we availed ourselves to it all. Even today, so many years later, I'm smiling as I write about those memories.

The next year, Tony moved off campus to an efficiency at the Stardust Motel. He was studying engineering and was determined to get good grades. I followed him off campus, and we were getting serious, but our parents intervened that summer, and our relationship ended. I was heartbroken that we were no longer together but went back to school in the fall to focus on attending my classes and studying.

Like many other colleges and universities had during this time, a sit-in took place in my dorm. We objected to the doors being locked by the resident assistants from midnight until six the next morning. I wish I could remember how we organized the protest, but I do remember the dean of the school attending and the lobby and stairs being filled with students. Our protest was successful. The dean called me into his office the next day and asked me to be one of the responsible students who would remain awake from midnight to 6 a.m. to open the doors throughout the night to other students coming and going. I agreed—even got a small stipend—and did that night duty for the rest of the semester. This was the first of what would be many organized political events I would later organize.

I do not remember why, but one day I needed to deliver something to a student in one of the men's dormitories. When he opened the door, the shirtless student who greeted me was about the tallest person I had ever seen—six feet, seven inches tall he would later tell me. I found myself staring at his chest and working my way up to his face. I had not seen him before on campus; he was a member of the basketball team, not someone who hung out with my group of friends. He was in good shape, with a chest that went on forever and broad shoulders that were magnificent specimens. He had reddish-brown hair and a smile on his face with a mustache that resembled Tom Selleck's. This was the first boy I had seen, since the breakup with Tony, who caught my eye. His name was Brent, and he and I would marry the following December. Brent graduated that spring, and although I would not have enough credits to graduate, I followed him to the Maryland suburbs of Washington, DC, where he had grown up.

Brent went to work with a construction company he had worked for the previous summers, and I got a job with a DC legislative law firm as their receptionist. Here, I was exposed to the world of politics, and I was thriving. After three years of marriage, it became clear to me we were growing in different directions. Upon reflection, Brent had been my rebound relationship from Tony. I remember my dad, while driving me to my wedding ceremony, telling me if I wasn't sure about this marriage, it wasn't too late to stop it. I started crying without really knowing why, and within several hours I was married. I am sorry about the way things ended, but had I not moved to DC with Brent, I might never have met the man I would be devoted to for the rest of our lives or discovered my love of politics.

PART TWO

# LIFE TOGETHER

# 2

---

# The Beginning
## *Not Just Cherry Trees Blossoming*

Springtime in Washington, DC, is marked by the blooming of the cherry blossoms, but in 1979 it also meant my life was taking a new direction, one that would pave the way for the next forty-two years.

It was early spring when Ron Platt and I, after a few friendly dinners, Washington Bullets basketball games, and political events, went on our first official date. I was working for the senior partner of the legislative law firm Ron retained to help lobby Congress on behalf of Burger King Corporation, headquartered in Miami. We enjoyed each other's company and had many dinners together over the winter months on his almost weekly trips to DC from Miami.

Our conversations were filled with our life stories—true and exaggerated—politics, family, laughs and hopes, all the things good friends talk about. Thanks to Ron's expense account, we were able to enjoy ourselves at many of the once famous and now long-gone restaurants DC political folks frequented. Our favorite was a French restaurant on K Street, where we would eat luscious French food and drink Grand Marnier. Its name, Romeo and Juliet, was a harbinger of where our friendship was headed. Every time we ate there, it seemed we would finish off dinner with a glass of Grand Marnier, and Ron would knock it over with his hand. Inevitably, it would spill on my dress and he would apologize, and we would always laugh.

As time went on in our long-distance friendship, a flame began to flicker. We would talk on the phone for hours in the evenings when Ron was in Miami and I was in DC. I wish I could remember what our talks were about, but neither of us ever ran out of things to say to the other. We both, it seemed, were aching for an understanding companion with whom to talk and laugh.

Washington, DC, can be a ridiculously small town. Political gossip always ran rampant, exposing any vulnerability, real or imagined. The stakes—money and power—were always high. The special comradery we had found was a comfort, a safe place together to share our fears, insecurities, hopes, and dreams, a true partner each could trust and believe in. At the time, neither of us was interested in a long-term romantic relationship, as we were each in the middle of a divorce. I worked for a prominent lawyer/lobbyist named Jerry Don Williams, J. D. as he was known, my first Washington job since leaving the University of Pittsburgh. He was the senior partner with a corner office, a desk with two phones and a phone installed in his car, along with a driver. Ron was an executive for Burger King Corporation, headquartered in Miami, and a client of J. D.'s firm. Ron and J. D. were both Oklahomans, and J. D. had been a mentor and longstanding friend of Ron's. In the 1970s, J. D. reinvented lobbying and became a powerhouse in political and social circles in Washington.

He was imposing in physical stature and personality, a man who would demand perfection and let you know when you did not achieve that mark. Few individuals at the time lasted long in J. D.'s orbit; he could be verbally explosive and highly intimidating. But somehow, we got along: I understood his motivation, even though it could be disconcerting, and he had confidence in my judgment in dealing with clients and members of Congress.

Unbeknownst to me, J. D. had noticed, or heard gossip more likely, that Ron and I were becoming friends, and he had matchmaking in mind when he suggested that Ron invite me for a weekend in Miami. Ron lost no time in suggesting such a trip, so off we flew for a romantic weekend together, both a little nervous.

When I first saw Ron, I found him attractive, and I can admit he was the first man whose butt I admired. He was smart, funny, and kind, and I found him to be quite sexy with his prematurely graying hair, piercing hazel eyes, and, of course, that great butt.

He was different from men I had found appealing previously, although he was the second cowboy I had been attracted to. Yes, he was good looking, but I was intrigued by the confidence of his manner and his demeanor. I loved the way he walked in his polished cowboy boots, his starched shirt, tie, and three-piece suit, like nothing could stop him. In addition to being kind, funny, and smart, he was supportive and encouraging in ways I had not experienced before in my first husband or any other relationships.

On the Saturday of our weekend together, Ron took me to see Burger King's corporate office building, with the big Whopper in the Sky logo on the building's roof. At the time, Ron's title at Burger King was vice president of corporate affairs, and he was proud of his first corporate job after years of running campaigns and teaching. He parked his corporate car—a red Camaro—in a space with his name painted on it. His big corner office with his nameplate on the door even had electric window blinds. His brag wall was covered with signed photos of politically powerful men shaking hands with him and smiling. I was so impressed.

Saturday night in Miami is time for clubbing, and that is exactly what we intended to do. We picked up Tony Borthick, a fellow Okie who worked with Ron, and off the three of us went in that red Camaro. Ron and Tony told funny political stories all night. Those were the days of Donna Summers hits and disco lights, so we danced to songs like "Hot Stuff," and we thought we were! When closing time came in the wee hours, Ron wanted to show me he was a gentleman so he opened the long Camaro door and helped me get in. Unfortunately, I was a little slow on the uptake, and when Ron slammed the door shut, my foot was still hanging outside.

Monday morning, we returned to DC, and I hobbled into the office on my swollen, black-and-blue foot. Rounding the corner to my office, I was met by J. D. Forever the gossip, J. D. wanted to hear how the "romantic" weekend had gone. When he saw me hobbling, he was aghast and called me into his office, closing the door behind him. I relayed the events of the weekend, particularly regarding my injured foot, as he sat back in his rocking chair puffing on his cigar. He said out of the side of his mouth, "Well, Susan, what did you expect from a boy from Oklahoma?"

Even though my foot was surely broken, it didn't matter. What mattered more was our exploring the beginnings of what could be real love. We laughed, we danced, we told stories, we talked about our hopes for the future, and we laughed some more. I thought this might be the beginning of a new life together, and so it was. We told the story of that first date many times over the years.

In late spring, I packed up my apartment, and Ron and I got in my Thunderbird, along with my dog, Chipper, a long-haired mutt, and drove to Miami. The trip took two days, and during that trip, we learned a lot more about each other; we knew a life together held promise. We had fallen in love, and our life together in Miami was settling into a natural, comfortable rhythm. After several months together, we knew we would marry—yes, he had already gotten on his knee and popped the question—but the timing was secondary to our personal commitment. Since we were already committed, we were not particularly concerned about the date; it was just a formality as far as we were concerned.

Meanwhile, we had only been living together in Miami for a month when Ron's seventeen-year-old daughter, Karen, said she wanted to come to Florida to live with her father. The only girl, she was the oldest of Ron's children. Karen had left her mother's home in Vanoss, Oklahoma, and had been living with Ron's parents in Ada, Oklahoma, until she graduated high school. She was ready to come live with us, or more importantly, her dad. She was as eager to escape Oklahoma as Ron had been at her age. This was the first time since she was a young girl that she lived with her father, and she clung to him. I am sure it was an exciting and scary time for her, as it was for me. She was immature and insecure for a seventeen-year-old, and even though she had never lived outside rural Oklahoma, she quickly acclimated to her new life in Florida. Ron had two other children; Keith, the older boy, lived with his mother in Vanoss, and the next year, he followed his sister to Florida to live with us and go to college. Like Karen, Keith adapted to life in Miami, joining the college baseball team, where he excelled. A third child, Martin, had died of SIDS many years earlier. Brent, the youngest of Ron's children at eight years old, was a product of his second marriage and lived with his mother in northern Virginia. He would come for visits in the summer months and on holidays, and we would see him on trips to Washington.

Ron spent most weeks flying to and from Washington when the Congress was in session, leaving Miami early on Tuesdays and usually returning home on Thursdays. Without Ron for most of the workweek, and now the stepmother of an insecure young woman who lived with us, I had no idea what I was doing. I was living in a new city, in a new relationship myself, and now was responsible for making sure Ron's kids were adapting and adjusting. I was scared about this new responsibility as a newlywed and stepmother at age twenty-five and knew his children might resent me, as I initially had my own stepmother. So I tried my best to be less a mother figure than a friend, hoping they would eventually come to accept and love me, the way I had come to treasure my stepmother.

Six months after I moved to Florida, we still had not felt an urgency to marry. In November, I got a job and became active in the local Democratic Party. Ron's usual busy travel schedule became even busier, as it was also election season. But it was also time for the Burger King Convention in San Francisco. I had never been to San Francisco, so I was excited to join Ron and a few thousand Burger King franchisees and their wives, corporate executives, and politicians. But there was a big fly in that ointment. As a corporate officer, Ron was told by his CEO it was inappropriate for him to have his girlfriend in the same hotel room. How times have changed since 1979. The solution was clear: we would get married and honeymoon at the Burger King

Convention! This would not necessarily be my dream honeymoon, but we would roll with it. However, the drama was just beginning.

As soon as we set the date, Senator Ted Kennedy's office called and asked Ron to set up political meetings in Miami; Kennedy was exploring a presidential run challenging President Carter in the Democratic Primary in 1980. Kennedy was scheduled to give a major speech to a ballroom-sized group of Miami business and political leaders in November. But time was running out before the start of the convention, so we had to move quickly. The new wedding date became November 8, one day after Kennedy's visit. These days were incredibly hectic for Ron. Not only did he have to prepare for the Burger King Convention, as senior vice president of corporate affairs, but he also had to help organize meetings for Kennedy and deal with the traveling press corps who accompanied the candidate—and get married.

The speech and visit were an incredible success, and next came the marriage ceremony. I cannot remember if we told our parents ahead of time, but Ron's folks were in Oklahoma and mine were in Richland, Washington; we didn't expect them to attend, as it wasn't the first marriage for either of us, and they knew we were committed to each other. Ron's boys were in school, so they would not be there. We made few plans since, in our mind, it was just confirmation of our commitment to each other. Ron enlisted the help of a coworker who was friends with a judge in Miami and arranged the time for the ceremony in the judge's chambers at the Miami courthouse. Our matchmaker friend in Washington, J. D. Williams, couldn't attend but wanted to send a representative, who flew down to witness and present the wedding gifts—copper pots, something quite special at the time. Ron's daughter, Karen, was excited to be there with her dad and share in the special day, so together we bought her a new dress to wear.

Finally, the wedding day arrived, and Ron woke with a huge swollen lump over his left eye. A visit to the doctor proved that an infection in a tear duct required lancing the eyelid to remove the infection. Once the medical issue was dealt with, all was ready. Ron, who always took pride in his appearance, appeared with a large gauze patch on his face from his left forehead across the eye to his right cheek. I wish we had photos from this event, but Ron objected to having his picture taken due to the patch across his face. Of course, many jokes ensued about why the black eye and the patch on the way to the wedding. I was serious about my new role as a corporate wife, so I wore a conservative gray suit from my closet. I'd had a big wedding and white dress the first time around, and none of that was important to me this time. Everyone was ready, so we all piled into the car for the trip to the judge's chambers in downtown Miami.

We arrived just in time for our appointment but found there would be one more delay. The judge was stuck in a contentious divorce proceeding, and no one knew how long it would take; it could extend to the next day. We were scheduled to fly to San Francisco the next day, so we cooled our heels and laughed about all the obstacles and mishaps. Luckily, the judge initiated a ten-minute recess from the divorce proceedings to marry us! The ceremony was remarkably simple. I don't remember exactly what we said; I know we made a commitment that we would never give up on each other. Having been married before, we knew the pain that divorce caused, and we swore never to do that again. Although we faced many tough times and challenges along the way, we kept that commitment to never give up on each other and never even considered breaking that pledge.

# 3

## Karen's Chance
## to Be a Hero

Ron and I were married just in time to celebrate Thanksgiving. We were living in Miami, and Karen was going to college there. The rest of our families lived across the country from Oklahoma to Pennsylvania and places in between. So, it was just the three of us, along with our retired racing greyhound, Rumble.

Even though I said I had not made up my mind about whether I wanted my own children, I instinctively knew I didn't. I suspect anyone who lost their mother in childhood will tell you how unsettling it is to grow up without a mother. We tend to be anxious and have a pervasive sense of foreboding that something awful is about to happen. When I married Ron, I got his three children as part of the package. I wasn't sure how I would adapt to being a stepmother, but I had my own stepmother to use as an example. The woman my father married, Barbara, was a godsend for both him and me. Although we dealt with the usual arguments and resentments, she would become someone who I loved and tried to emulate with Ron's children. I wanted to be someone they felt they could talk to and hoped I could be a welcoming figure for them. It was harder for me to relate to Keith than to Karen, as he was a teenage boy, and I had no idea what drove him. But I gave it my best shot with all three kids.

I had never cooked a turkey before but was looking forward to our first real Thanksgiving as a newly blended family. I talked to Barb about how best to cook the turkey, and Ron consulted his mother about how to make Oklahoma cornbread dressing. I rose early on Thanksgiving morning to begin the preparations. Once I dressed the turkey and put it in the oven, it was time to prepare all the side dishes, including a new recipe for jalapeño-spiced cranberry sauce, along with sweet potatoes, green beans, and pecan and pumpkin pies. Ron would make the dressing with drippings from the turkey. In my family, we stuffed the turkey, but Ron's family made dressing in a separate pan. Who knew?

Everything was going according to my careful plan until I noticed an unpleasant odor that seemed to be overwhelming the kitchen. The smells I remembered from my childhood Thanksgivings were so enticing they made your mouth water, and you could not wait for dinner to be served. But this was not that same mouthwatering smell. I assumed the smell was coming from the garbage, so I asked Ron to take the trash outside. He readily did so, then sprayed Lysol around the room, but the smell persisted.

When it came time to baste the turkey, I opened the oven door and saw it was a beautiful golden color. Pleased with myself, I basted the turkey, and as I began closing the oven door, I discovered the reason for the odor. I slammed the oven door and ran screaming bloody murder out the front door, waving the large basting spoon. Ron came running behind me to see what I was screaming about. When I finally caught my breath and calmed down enough to speak, I told him what I had seen in the oven: a shriveled-up mouse, in the sitting position, staring straight at me through dead, beady eyes. I then discovered Ron hated mice about as much as I did and said there was no way he was going to remove its shriveled body from the oven.

After a little thinking, Ron produced a plan to remove the mouse carcass from the oven. He went to Karen's bedroom to see if she was awake yet. I listened as he told her the story about the unfortunate mouse and the turkey. I could hear her giggles as she heard the story, and she agreed to help, leaving her glasses behind. Karen's mother lived on a farm in Vanoss, an even more rural town than Ada, so Karen was used to dealing with animals of all kinds. In her nightgown, without her glasses, and with a smile on her face and a certain twinkle of mischief in her eye, she came downstairs to save Turkey Day. Karen had the best giggle I have ever heard, and proudly stated through those giggles that she would remove the carcass from the oven. So, with spatula in hand, she opened the oven door, scraped that mouse off the bottom of the oven, and tossed it in the trash outside.

There was just no way I could eat that turkey, but Karen and Ron ate it up, and this first Thanksgiving dinner would long be remembered. Ron loved to tell that story year after year at Thanksgiving. So, in memory of our wonderful, shared Thanksgivings together I retell that story, adding a word of caution to be sure to check your oven before you cook your Thanksgiving turkey.

# 4

## The Ever-Changing Nature of a Career in Politics and the Reagan Revolution

In the first eight months of 1980, life was good for us in Miami. Ron and I were active in the Kennedy for President campaign (Ron served nationally and me locally), and we were becoming a better known couple in the local business, arts, and political communities. Because of his position at Burger King, Ron served on several local boards, ranging from those of a modern dance company to Florida International University. When Ron was not lobbying in Washington, our weekends were filled with social and political events representing the corporation, a major philanthropic donor in Miami, often with our names and photos appearing in the society pages.

Karen was attending Florida State University but returned home after several girls around the campus had been found murdered. We learned later they were victims of serial killer Ted Bundy. She then enrolled at Florida International University. And when summer arrived,

Ron's older son Keith moved in with us, to attend FIU and play baseball.

That summer I was asked by the chairman of the Democratic National Committee (DNC) to host the first fundraiser for the newly created Women's Division of the DNC. It was a first for me to head up an event like this, and I was terribly anxious at age twenty-five to organize and host this first event, but with a lot of help, it was a great success.

As August approached, I was looking forward to attending my first Democratic National Convention, held in New York's Madison Square Garden. I had only been active in Democratic politics for a brief time, while Ron had been involved since his college days at the University of Oklahoma. Senator Ted Kennedy was challenging President Jimmy Carter for the nomination, and we were big supporters of Kennedy, since President John Kennedy had been the impetus for Ron's involvement in politics. And later, when Ron was teaching political science at Lamar State University in Texas, he became president of Texans for Robert Kennedy for President.

While I remember only a couple specifics from that convention, I do remember standing on the floor of the convention, having somehow secured credentials, mesmerized as Senator Kennedy delivered his concession speech. I remember the packed convention hall being so quiet you could hear a pin drop; you could feel the simmering electricity of anticipation about what he would say. The deal was done; President Carter would be our nominee again, and the speech would be important for the Democratic Party and the delegates in attendance to unify and support Carter.

"The work goes on, the cause endures, the hope still lives, and the dream shall never die."[1] His speech was spellbinding, one of the most memorable political speeches in modern politics—a concession speech that laid out his belief in America's potential for greatness and his hopes for the future. It had such an impact on me that if I hadn't already been engaged in the political process, it would have cemented my work life for the rest of my career. He captured the emotion of the moment: commitment, courage, and belief in democratic ideals. We deeply believed in what he spoke about; his hopes were our hopes for opportunity, equality, and fairness for all citizens.

On November 4, 1980, President Carter lost the election to Ronald Reagan by a ten-point margin. For the first time in twenty-five years, Republicans won back the majority of the US Senate by a net gain of twelve seats. The Democrats would still control the US House of Representatives, but they lost many seats. Many believe that the 1980 election, the Reagan Revolution as it was called, began a shift to the right for the country.

We were four days shy of our first wedding anniversary on Election Day, but we didn't feel much like celebrating. Not long after, we would find that not only did the power shift in Washington, but it also shifted throughout corporate America. And it meant that Ron, a Democrat, was out of his corporate job, replaced by a Republican.

Thus, we began our move back to Washington. We put our house on the market, but with mortgage interest rates averaging around 15 percent, it was going to be a hard sell. We rented an apartment for Karen and Keith, both still at Florida International University. Karen understood, but Keith felt we were abandoning him. This was his first time living with his father in years, and now he was leaving again. We understood how he felt, but there was nothing we could do about it. Ron was more likely to find work in Washington. So, we packed up the car with our dog, Rumble, and drove back to Washington.

My old boss J. D. Williams helped us find a tiny town-house on Capitol Hill to rent. The townhouse was on South Capitol Street, one block from the House office buildings and right next to the train tracks. That townhouse shook many times during the day and night, a fitting metaphor for what we were living through.

I was naïve, but I had great confidence Ron would find work and we could rebuild. And I was right. A small Republican lobbying firm brought him on to help with the Democrats. It was not ideal for him, but we were glad he found work so fast when few Democrats could find a job in a town now controlled by Republicans. A Democratic congressman hired me as his scheduler, and I worked in the Rayburn House Office Building, a one-block commute from our townhouse.

What a difference an election makes! Reality hit home for me: our careers and success depended on our politics, not our abilities. If I had not understood it before, I certainly did then. One minute we were living in Miami with an expense account, and the next, we had no income with a mortgage, two kids in college, and child support for another. I was twenty-six years old, and Ron was thirty-eight. We had to figure out what we would do while waiting for the Democrats to win back the White House and the Senate. After a short time, Ron's reputation as a smart, tenacious advocate for his clients led to a job with a prominent Democratic law firm, and thus began his distinguished lobbying career. I started my political work with several jobs in congressional offices in the House of Representatives, the last one as a chief of staff for a congressman from New Jersey on the powerful Ways and Means Committee.

We were back in Washington, working to establish ourselves and our careers in Washington, while also building a solid foundation for our marriage and family. There was no time for vacations or slacking off. When it wasn't work, work, work, we made time for special moments of togetherness with a dinner out or going to the movies. When we did travel, it was to see Ron's folks in Oklahoma and mine, who were in Tennessee at the time. Since Ron's youngest son, Brent, lived in the Virginia suburbs with his mother, we saw him frequently. So, while we had an extended family, they lived in different parts of the country, and we were very much "just us two" most of the time, the time needed in any long-term committed marriage to develop better understanding of who we were together and what each of us needed individually. During our first two years of marriage, we'd had Ron's daughter and then his son sharing our lives, and at times I wondered if I could manage the many needs.

We worked hard and saved enough money to buy a late 1800s four-story townhouse on 3rd Street NE on Capitol Hill, one block from the Senate office buildings. From our bedroom, we could see the top of the Capitol above the weeping cherry tree in front of our house. I loved that house with its working fireplace on each floor, original marble facades, and original pine floors complete with leaning pine steps. Ron's and my folks all thought we were crazy to buy that townhouse, but it ended up being a very smart thing to do for our homelife and our careers. Being so close to Capitol Hill afforded us precious time together. We would often walk to local restaurants just one or two blocks away.

Ron loved it too, but for different reasons. Even though Ron had grown up in rural Oklahoma, he loved living in the city. He used to say he was happiest feeling the concrete between his toes! Ron loved the feeling of excitement and success that living on Capitol Hill represented. And it was the perfect place to host fundraising receptions for our favorite politicians and candidates.

By this time, Ron's older son, Keith, had left Miami to continue his education at the University of Oklahoma. Oklahoma had been his home for most of his childhood, and it was where his mother and stepfather had their farm. By 1985, while attending college in Miami, Karen had fallen in love and was planning a wedding in Ada, Oklahoma. Several years after that, Keith would also marry in Oklahoma.

One thing Ron told me from the beginning of our relationship was that his kids would always come first. Initially, this was difficult for me to accept. He explained that I was the love of his life, but he was responsible for his children, and he would never abdicate that responsibility. He took that responsibility so seriously that when he and his first wife divorced after the death of their youngest boy from SIDS, he tried to ensure he would at least have shared custody of his children. But at that time in the seventies, shared custody was virtually unheard of. He would be responsible for child support and have specifically prescribed times for visitation. So, Ron had left for Washington, DC, where he could earn a better living than he could teaching school.

By now, we were financially stable, and when the time came for both Karen and Keith to buy their first home, Ron supplied the down payments. Karen was settled in Miami with her husband, and Keith with his wife moved to Dallas. Ron believed he should do what he could to give his kids a solid start in their new life. Riddled with guilt about divorcing their mother, he blamed himself for any of their shortcomings. He was tough as nails when it came to business, but when it came to his children and family, he was a soft, fuzzy pillow. Ron let his kids know he would always be there for them, and he was; he always answered their calls with understanding and kindness.

At times I was jealous of how openly Ron expressed his love for his children. These were the times I wished my own father would say out loud that he loved me. My father often showed me his love by his actions, but it wasn't until late in the eighties that I told him during a rare argument that I was hurt he never said he loved me. A few months later, he came to Washington for a visit, and he hugged me and told me he loved me. Watching Ron with his children gave me the courage to confront my feelings and verbalize them to the person who had meant the most to me for so long.

Our first grandchild, Kristin, was born to Karen and her husband in August 1988. It was a joyous time. Loaded with gifts, we flew to Miami to meet her as soon as she was home from the hospital. Ron was proud of the life Karen was making for herself and her new family. I remember the smile on his face when he held Kristin for the first time and proclaimed he wanted to be called Paw-Paw, the name his children had called his father. Several years later when Kristin could talk, she determined I would be called Su-Su, and it stuck.

Ron was now in partnership with Ed Rollins, President Reagan's campaign manager, and several others, and the new business was doing well. Ed had bought a house on High Knob Mountain in the Blue Ridge Mountains outside Front Royal, Virginia, in addition to a couple other prominent Republicans. We visited one weekend and decided to buy property there as well and build a weekend home. Ron's folks could live there full time, sixty miles away from us on Capitol Hill. I was on a break from politics and became responsible for overseeing the design and building of that home.

Ron's parents sold their home in Ada, and I flew out to drive them to their new home in Virginia. They were ready to be closer to their only child, and we could go there to relax and recharge on the weekends and holidays. The home had three bedrooms with two master suites, on the side of the mountain with a beautiful view on three decks of the Blue Ridge Mountains.

The only time we would travel to Oklahoma after that would be to return his parents to their home for burial after their deaths and to attend one Oklahoma Sooners football game.

# 5

## Surrounded by Snakes

Ron was a natural politician with knowledge and experience. I was just beginning to put my toes in the water, but I knew that politics was to be the focus of my career. We quickly joined the other Washingtonians on the political circuit and began hosting regular fundraisers for members of Congress in our home.

Our first ten years of marriage were all about building a solid foundation and increasing in confidence for our marriage, our extended family, and our careers. Professionally, it was an exciting time, one that exceeded many of our expectations, but our family also faced serious issues during this decade.

Ron's daughter's and son's families grew, and everyone seemed to be thriving. Ron's folks were happily living in our home on High Knob Mountain growing vegetables and enjoying the weekends with us. My parents had retired to Virginia, about twenty miles from High Knob, and we saw them regularly. We had regular family gatherings, and the kids and grandkids visited several times a year. We were grateful to have both sets of parents close by. Ron's folks even introduced my Pittsburgh parents to chicken fried steak and okra, and they loved it. We were all stable and happy.

I was offered a job managing a congressional race for the son of an old friend of Ron's. The office was in Winchester, about twenty miles from Front Royal and forty miles from DC, so the location worked well. I was beside myself with excitement and fear. I knew I wanted to manage a campaign, but I had no experience in doing so and no idea where to begin. I knew a manager needed to be a leader, organized, strategic, trustworthy, and level-headed when the inevitable crises arose—skills I possessed. But I lacked the specifics. Ron, on the other hand, had run many campaigns, even a couple in Virginia. The process all came naturally to him. Each night we talked about what I needed to do. Ron was a good teacher; he helped me develop a budget, a plan for staffing and fundraising, ideas for polling and messaging, and ideas to get out the vote. We made a good team. I discovered something about campaigns, though: they never run on time. That meant I was always running late too.

One Saturday afternoon, I was racing up High Knob Mountain after a campaign event to meet Ron for dinner, and I was thirty minutes late. Because Ron's parents had gone back to Oklahoma for a visit, we had the house to ourselves and were looking forward to enjoying a quiet romantic dinner for two with a soak in the hot tub. Since this was 1990, before the appearance of cell phones, I couldn't call to tell him I was on my way. I barreled down the driveway, came to a screeching stop, and bolted toward the house. I pictured him waiting in the hot tub, with the water getting cool and the wine getting warm.

As I approached, I heard moaning coming from inside the house. I ran in to discover Ron on the bathroom floor with a towel wrapped around his foot. He said a snake had bitten him on his foot when he was getting in the hot tub on the lower deck. He was amazingly calm but sweating profusely and in quite a bit of pain. I, on the other hand, immediately entered panic mode. This was real and profoundly serious, and I knew we needed help and quickly. I was sure you had thirty minutes to get medical attention after a poisonous snake bite, and since I was thirty minutes late, I thought we were in real trouble.

I helped him into the car and raced down the mountain to the hospital in Front Royal, a good twenty minutes away. Ron kept telling me to slow down, that I would kill us on the way to the hospital, but I kept thinking about those thirty minutes.

Finally, at the entrance to the emergency room, I slammed on the brakes, threw the car into park, jumped out, and dashed in to get help. I told them my husband had been bitten by a snake, and his foot was swelling quickly. They came running with a stretcher and took him into one of the treatment rooms. I cannot remember the last time I was that scared; I honestly believed he might die because I had been late.

A man in a white coat, who I assumed to be a doctor assigned to Ron, approached me. He had questions: How long ago had Ron been bitten? What kind of snake? And more, many of which I could not answer.

A short while later, a different doctor approached me. He said he had been called in to treat Ron because he had trained at Methodist Hospital in San Antonio, Texas, and had treated numerous snakebite patients. I was finally beginning to calm down. He told me thirty minutes was only a magic number for rattlesnake bites. The concern was more about the swelling at this point.

Ron wasn't sure if the snake was a copperhead, and the doctor wanted me to find out. When the snake had reared up to bite again, Ron had hit it with a piece of wood and thrown it off the deck. The doctor instructed me to go back up the mountain and search for that snake. Oh, God. So once again, I raced up the mountain and enlisted the help of a neighbor. Cautiously, gingerly, and quickly, we searched the back property, more than one acre, for the snake, to no avail. We had to assume the snake that bit Ron had been a poisonous copperhead. Back down the mountain to the hospital I raced. My ability to be calm in a crisis was clearly being tested!

Based on Ron's description of the snake and the swelling that occurred, everyone agreed it must have been a copperhead, and the treatment was antivenom. The hospital had none in stock, and someone was dispatched to the regional hospital in Winchester that verified they had several doses of the treatment. So, we waited a little longer. They had now moved Ron to a room on the PCU wing (progressive care unit). They had him hooked up to a heart monitor, as snake venom can cause several serious cardiovascular effects, including cardiac arrest, atrial fibrillation, and myocardial infarction. My fear once again went off the charts. His entire leg was now swelling, and there was concern the inflammation would reach his testicles and swell so much that the skin would need to be surgically cut to prevent the death of his leg or more.

By the time the antivenom arrived, Ron's snake-bit ankle was the size of his thigh (possibly an exaggeration, but not by much). He also faced possible side effects from the antivenom, the most common of which was nausea, but sometimes patients experienced delayed development of transitory arthritis and increased blood pressure. And, of course, he would later develop both.

Ron received two antivenom treatments. The swelling slowed, eliminating the need for surgery on his leg, stopping just below his testicles. After three days in the hospital, he was released. Within weeks thereafter, I hired a small company named Snakebusters to scour the area around our home; they found and removed six more copperheads. Ron became the subject of a regional AP story about his saga and our snake removal. Of course, I knew Ron was one in a million, but who knew he would be one of one hundred copperhead snakebite victims that year in Virginia.

Word spread around Capitol Hill, and, as usual, Ron was on the phone with well-wishers, telling jokes about whose bite was worse, the snake's or those on Capitol Hill. So, with cane in hand, Ron had another delightful story to tell. And even though my candidate would not win the election, I loved the challenge, the pressure, the fast pace, and the camaraderie of a campaign. And now, thanks to Ron, I had another skill to add to my resume.

# 6

## Losses and Gains

In early 1991, Ron's mother, now in her late seventies, had a recurrence of breast cancer from years earlier. The cancer returned to her liver, and we soon realized that she would not survive long, even with chemotherapy. In late May of 1992, after losing consciousness, she was taken by ambulance to the hospital, where for a week we took turns spending the night in a bed next to hers, until she died on a morning when Ron's dad was with her. Ron had a complicated relationship with his mother, but he was there for her and his father during this time. We and all her grandchildren made our way to Oklahoma to lay her to rest. Ron said little about her passing, but his relationship with his father grew much stronger as time went on.

During this time, we checked on and visited Ron's dad as often as we could, and my folks and our neighbors helped with that as well. He continued to live on the mountain with his little dog Poo for company. He fed Poo a piece of

Hershey's chocolate every night, even though we told him repeatedly that chocolate was not good for dogs.

While we were grieving the loss of Ron's mother, new career opportunities presented themselves for both of us. Although my first job as campaign manager running a congressional race ended in defeat for the candidate, I had done a respectable job as his campaign manager. I loved the work and knew I had found my niche.

With the help of a friend of Ron's, I got my next job with Senator Charles Robb serving as chair of the Democratic Senatorial Campaign Committee during the 1991–1992 election cycle. I loved it. My job was managing the large events for the House and Senate fundraising dinners, as well as planning and overseeing the events for the Senate at the Democratic National Convention in New York City to nominate Governor Bill Clinton for president. I was accompanied by my local aide-de-camp, Bryson Monteleone, who was not even twenty-one years old when he hitched on to my wagon. Although Bryson was young and inexperienced, he had the desire, work ethic, and humor that melded well with mine.

I was responsible for organizing the Democratic National Convention for the United States Senate at Madison Square Garden in New York in mid-July 1992. Ron had been traveling with Senator Tom Harkin during the presidential primary process, but when Harkin dropped out, we all supported Governor Bill Clinton. Ron was getting the itch for campaigns again but knew he could not leave his job. Luckily, Ron's firm saw the benefit of his campaigning for a month or so for Clinton, and so did his clients. Off Ron went to

Kentucky to campaign for Clinton, and I went to Pennsylvania for the Democratic Senatorial Campaign Committee.

I took many trips to New York City with all the bells and whistles of police escorts through New York traffic and special security credentials. I began to travel for the Committee to do political organizing work in other states occasionally and was even able to spend time organizing in my home state of Pennsylvania for a special Senate election.

At the largest and final fundraising dinner of the year for the Senate, I was able, with the help of Senator Carl Levin of Michigan, to secure Aretha Franklin, the Queen of Soul, to be the performer. What a hoot it was to watch her perform while Senator Joe Biden and many others threw red roses from their table onto the stage when she finished her last song.

At the end of her performance, her aide approached me on the dance floor and said Ms. Franklin wanted to see me. I was a little concerned she was upset about something as I followed the aide backstage. But Aretha asked, "Did I do okay? Did they enjoy my performance?" Of course, my response to her was that I had never seen so many senators standing and throwing roses on stage for a performer.

The next morning one of her staff phoned to invite me to meet her in her hotel room at the Willard. We had to finalize the business of payment for her performance, and she wanted to be paid in cash. She met me at the door, still in her bathrobe, and asked me to join her for tea. We had a great conversation, and I found her to be warm and down-to-earth. When I left, I felt like I was floating on air for days. What a story I had to tell.

When the campaigns ended, with Democrats as winners, Ron and I traveled to St. Martin in the Caribbean. We reserved a small beach house with its own pool and clothing-optional beach. The latter was not something we discovered until we got there, and Ron teased me mercilessly about whether a good Catholic girl like me would at least take off my top! We loved these trips together. Our only activity, other than going to the beach, was going out for dinner. We loved tasting all the great dishes at the French-Caribbean restaurants in the nearby town of Marigot. And later, when we got more adventurous, we went tandem parasailing. The laid-back atmosphere was exactly what we needed to recover from the stress of our jobs.

When we returned from our vacation, it was December and time for Christmas and then the inauguration of President Bill Clinton. An exciting time for Democrats in Washington, we attended every ball and party we could, joining in the celebration. I was planning my next job with Senator Robb, and Ron was bringing in new clients to his firm. It was an enjoyable time to be a Democrat.

In January of 1993, Senator Robb's leadership of the DSCC was ending, meaning his staff would be out of jobs; Robb also faced reelection in 1994. The DSCC had raised more money in the previous election cycle than ever before and was able to help maintain the fourteen-seat majority in the Senate, five of whom were women. Never had that many women been elected to the Senate, and it became known as the "year of the woman." We were all proud of that accomplishment. But this period had also been challenging for Robb's own political career. Rumors persisted of his attendance at parties at Virginia Beach where drugs and women had been present. He was facing reelection after being under investigation by a grand jury for political tricks and illegally taped conversations. A month after Robb was scheduled to appear before the grand jury, in early January of 1993, they chose not to indict him. It was a momentous day and a relief to all of us. But newspaper stories continued to report that he had received a "massage" by a former Miss Virginia. As this was contrary to his spit-and-polish Marine image, his political career was at a crossroads and his popularity was in the toilet. None of us could imagine how his wife, Lynda, the daughter of President Lyndon Johnson, was dealing with the onslaught of media coverage.

At this time, I saw an opportunity. Looking back on it now, my decision seems both bold and delusional. I decided I wanted to become Senator Robb's campaign manager for his reelection campaign in 1994. I didn't dwell on the fact that I had only run one political campaign—and lost it! Nor did I consider the fact that this was going to become one of the highest-profile races in the country in 1994. Few campaign staffers wanted to jump into that campaign. The once shiny Marine was now publicly tarnished, but I had already worked for him for two years. I respected him and Lynda, and I wanted to take on the challenge because I felt I could help him win.

With Ron's encouragement, I drafted a long memo to Senator Robb detailing how I would help him win the election. I worked for days on that memo, writing and rewriting steps I believed needed to be taken to rehabilitate his name and win reelection. Several days after sending him the memo, Robb called me into his senate office to discuss his thoughts about my memo. In January of 1993, following Bill Clinton's inauguration as president, I was hired to lead Robb's reelection effort, and Bryson and I set up our office under the indoor pool at the Robbs' McLean home (Bryson dubbed it "the bunker"). We often joked about being in the basement, but where else would we have been visited by Lynda Johnson Robb and former First Lady, Lady Bird Johnson?

Another attraction of being in the Robbs' home was the opportunity to regularly sample the treats prepared by Tony Townes. The Robbs had convinced Tony to leave his position as chef for the governor when Robb's term ended and come work for them in McLean as their private chef. Tony's brownies were a particular favorite of Senator Robb, and he would occasionally share with us. We all loved Tony, who provided much irreverent comic relief with his stories.

When I was first hired in 1993, all experienced and highly regarded political prognosticators and analysts believed Robb's odds of winning reelection were slim to none. Analysts ranging from the University of Virginia's Dr. Larry Sabato to the famed political analyst and election forecaster Charlie Cook, founder of The Cook Political Report, agreed his prospects were poor. In addition to political analysts, news reporters from all news outlets predicted Robb's chances for victory were poor.

Ron's firm had an office in London, and they asked him to travel there to speak to clients in the United Kingdom about the incoming Clinton Administration. He never had the bug for international travel before, but knowing I did, he accepted, and I went along for the ride. Before the trip, a visit to the doctor showed Ron's blood pressure was way too high. He was given medication and instructions to return to the doctor once we were back from London. The medication didn't seem to help, so he underwent several tests that revealed that after kidney stone surgery in the eighties, scar tissue had formed, blocking the tube from his kidney. Ron asked me to meet him at the Democratic Club for drinks. While there, he calmly told me he needed to have one kidney removed; he then made a joke that, since he had two, it wouldn't be a problem.

We got this diagnosis at about the time Senator Robb asked me to run his reelection campaign, and it was not going to be an easy job. I felt the pressure of the new job and concern for my husband, but I followed Ron's example and did my best to remain calm and optimistic. Within a week after that, Ron was in the hospital preparing to have the one nonfunctioning kidney removed. The surgical team told me the procedure would last about three hours. After four and a half hours, I called my folks to ask them to join me at the hospital, as I was beside myself with worry. Just as my parents arrived at the surgery waiting room, Ron's surgeon came out to tell me the surgery was difficult because the nonfunctioning kidney was plastered to surrounding organs. But the other kidney was functioning as it should, and Ron should be fine. Since he was just over fifty at the time, his other kidney would not grow to take on the new load, but the surgeon said he should live a normal life span if he took care of the remaining kidney. This meant drinking lots of water, something I constantly reminded him to do. As usual, Ron wouldn't be down for long and was only home a few days before he returned to work. I don't know how he did it, as the incision was over a foot long, but he was strong and determined.

By the fall of 1993, Ron was ready for a change, and he suggested moving off Capitol Hill to Great Falls, Virginia, about twenty miles outside the District. Great Falls is a bucolic village, with homes on at least three acres of land, surrounded by both a national and a county park along the Potomac River. We were both ready for a more peaceful place to relax after our high-pressure days, and Great Falls would be perfect for that. We found a home on five acres of land at the end of a road that surrounded the park. It was secluded, had a fabulous stone fireplace, cathedral-ceiling great room, and a sunroom with a hot tub (I think the hot tub sold Ron on this home). I loved it as well; surrounded by deer and nature, the setting always calmed me. We bought that house, sold our house on Capitol Hill, and moved before Christmas 1993, right before the Robb for Senate Campaign would really heat up.

That year, 1993, was intended to be about Senator Robb getting back to senate business and being out of the front pages for grand jury visits and scandal. The campaign, meanwhile, was charged with reaching out to the grassroots network of Democrats and their organizations, endeavoring to reconnect them with Robb in the same way they connected when his approval numbers were in the high 70 percent range. And, of course, we were trying to raise enough money to wage a vigorous campaign. Three issues that came before the Senate made organizing the grassroots supporters even more difficult: Clinton had promised action on allowing gays and lesbians to serve openly in the military, and Robb agreed with this position, but most Virginians disagreed. Next, Robb would not support a joint resolution proposing a constitutional amendment to ban flag burning. And third, he was in favor of banning weapons of war from being sold to ordinary citizens, a position that incurred wrath from the National

Rifle Association and many more Virginians. Since Robb was fully behind all of Clinton's agenda, our first fundraising letter to Virginians was from President Clinton supporting Senator Robb and asking Virginia Democrats to join him.

Our challenges in the Robb campaign became even more apparent by Thanksgiving 1993. The gubernatorial campaign in Virginia had just ended, and our Democratic nominee, Virginia's first statewide-elected female official, Mary Sue Terry, got shellacked by Congressman George Allen, son of the famous coach of the Washington Redskins. Since we were not getting enthusiastic support from many of the ten Democratic Congressional District Chairs, I suggested to Robb we invite them to his home for dinner with him and Lynda. All those invited accepted the invitation, coming from all parts of the state to attend. Lynda helped carry the conversation at the table, and everyone was enjoying their meal. Toward the end of the dinner, Senator Robb began speaking about the upcoming race and asked them directly for their support. While I hadn't believed their support would be unanimous, I was shocked that only two of the ten were ready to commit, a precarious position to be in if you are a sitting senator.

I had quit smoking years before, but now I resembled a chimney. Poor Bryson would have to fight his way, coughing, through the cloud of smoke billowing out of my windowless office daily.

In January of 1994, Oliver North, a Republican, officially announced his candidacy for Senate, and we finally moved out of the bunker into a close-by office building. We were a ragtag, tight-knit group of committed staffers who put our noses to the grindstone and blocked out everything but our mission to win. Along with Bryson, I hired Chris Elliott, who would be Robb's driver; Chris Long and Tom

Nagle, experienced fundraisers, were charged with fundraising activities. We hired Bert Rohrer as the campaign press secretary, in addition to senate staff press secretary Peggy Wilhide. After a call from former governor and presidential nominee Michael Dukakis, I hired John DiBiase as our most capable advance person and all-around funny man. Lisa Pratt was hired to assist Lynda on speeches and campaign travel across Virginia. Mike Henry, who worked for the Democratic Legislative Caucus at the time, was hired as field director. Tom Lehner was hired to be Robb's chief of staff in the Senate, and along with Susan Albert, who helped with our scheduling, and Ridge Schuyler, Tom led all legislative priorities; many other present and former Robb staffers added immensely to our efforts.

In light of the Democrats' loss in the statewide governor and attorney general races, combined with Robb's grand jury investigation and discussions of his extracurricular activities, political gossip was rampant that the current governor, L. Douglas Wilder, the first African American governor in the United States, and often a foil to Robb, would announce a run to challenge him in the Democratic primary. On January 12, at his final State of the Commonwealth Address and after great anticipation and drama, Wilder announced he would not challenge Robb in the primary. We all let out a major sigh of relief.

One of the first things I learned about campaigns was to address your vulnerabilities first. So, our first big event after Wilder's announcement was a Women for Robb event. With the former Miss Virginia, Tai Collins, claiming she had an affair with Robb, we felt we had to show that Lynda and their three girls were behind him and his reelection. Organizers of the event for women included former First Lady Lady Bird Johnson, and political icon Barbara Jordan of Texas, the first African American woman elected to the United States House of Representatives from the South. All prominent female Democratic leaders were now on board. It certainly was not lost on anyone that a woman, the first in Virginia and in a minority around the country, was also managing his campaign.

Although Governor Wilder was not going to challenge us in the primary, which we won by a large margin, Wilder would deliver boxloads of petitions to get on the November ballot as an independent.

Headlines and stories about the race appeared in national newspapers and on television reports. Our Republican opponent, Lt. Col. Oliver North, already a national figure, was the darling of the Republicans' "new conservatism," and he was raising money hand over fist. We, on the other hand, were struggling to conserve our money. Robb was no longer viewed as the clean-cut rising star, and many wallets remained closed for our race.

In addition to Wilder and North, former Virginia Attorney General Marshall Coleman, formerly a Republican, would enter the race as an independent endorsed by Virginia's other US Senator, Republican John Warner. Now we would have to manage a four-way race with one Republican and two Independents. At about this time, early summer, I was approached by a young filmmaker named R. J. Cutler who was intent on documenting this historic race. We determined it would not be in Robb's best interest to allow him behind the scenes in our campaign, and Robb agreed. Robb had been through enough negative headlines and stress in the last several years, and it was beginning to show in his campaigning demeanor. He was reticent and sluggish, and he wasn't getting enough sleep. North's campaign loved the attention and welcomed them behind the scenes as they played to the cameras.

Robb traveled the Commonwealth throughout August, visiting thirty-eight cities and all ninety-five counties in a whirlwind tour. Robb never spent a night in a hotel room, always staying in supporters' homes, where he felt more comfortable and could have a good discussion with them. Monday, September 5, was Labor Day, and the following day, Robb would debate all three opponents, moderated by Judy Woodruff with CNN. The venue was Hampden-Sydney College, a private men's college ninety miles southwest of Richmond. Robb was prepared for all issue questions by the staff, but we had to decide, and he would have to agree, how to respond to attacks about grand juries, beauty queens, and parties. We settled on saying "I have some chinks in my armor" and leave it at that. We hoped. When we arrived at Hampden-Sydney, it became apparent our supporters would be greatly outnumbered when several busloads of young men arrived, in addition to all the men who attended the college and filed into the Hall.

About halfway through the debate, the candidates began getting questions about how to get the federal budget deficit under control and what cuts, if any, should be made to entitlement programs like Medicare and Social Security. In a moment of utter exasperation, Senator Robb responded, "I would take food from the mouths of widows and orphans if we had to, to begin to solve this problem, and I know that's a very provocative line, but it's the only way to solve the problem." To which Wilder responded, "It's a stupid line."

North's team jumped on Robb's statement, and by the next day, they produced "Widows and Orphans for North" bumper stickers. I cringed every time I saw one of those signs on the back bumper of a car. Within a week of that debate, Governor Wilder would withdraw from the race, stating he was a realist and "knew when to hold and when to fold." With the help of President Clinton, we were able to arrange a meeting between Senator Robb and Governor Wilder shortly thereafter, where Wilder told Robb he was dropping out and would endorse him.

In late September, Oliver North criticized Robb's military service, calling him an "8th and I" Marine (referencing the military complex on Capitol Hill where many of the ceremonial events in Washington involving Marines took place) and saying Robb had not been involved in active combat. In fact, Robb had served in combat in Vietnam, so this challenge went straight to his core as a Marine.

I had begun hearing from many of our supporters who were upset that Robb refused to respond to North's many attacks, most of which were untrue. When Robb next came to the campaign office, I told him I wanted him to respond vehemently to these attacks in a press conference. But Robb declined to say anything publicly. I approached him again in the parking lot as he left our offices and told him not only was I getting calls from supporters, but the entire staff was wondering why he was not responding to such a frontal attack on who he was at his core. I was a little surprised at myself for expressing our beliefs so strongly, but it worked: he looked at me and said, "Set it up." I did not usually attend these events; Peggy Wilhide, our press secretary, had that duty. But I attended this event, held at the Marine Barracks at 8th and I Streets in Southwest DC. I stood next to him at the podium, holding his military record, which was at least three inches thick. At the appropriate time in his statement, he grabbed the record out of my hand, threw it down on the podium with a loud noise, and proclaimed, "I am no longer going to let North get away with the deceptions that have taken place ... he has had real problems with the truth and lied about my record." I went back to a jubilant campaign headquarters, where I remember saying to the staff, "Fasten your seat belts; the gloves have finally come off."

We were in the final month of the campaign where rumors and misdirection were rampant, and no one was surprised by anything that would happen next. In my time as campaign manager, I had never been directly attacked, as far as I knew, until G. Gordon Liddy, of the Nixon Watergate break-in scandal, now a right-wing radio talk-show host, wondered on his national show if in addition to my role as campaign manager, I had also, like the Virginia beauty pageant winner, had a personal relationship with Robb. I was incensed, as was Ron. The best advice I got on how to manage this situation came from none other than Lynda Robb. She told me her mother taught her in these kinds of circumstances not to respond; just walk with your head high and let it flow off your back. So, I followed her great advice, and that is what I did.

By the third week in October, with a little more than two weeks left in the campaign, a public poll was released showing North leading Robb by four points. President Clinton then appeared at a unity event in Northern Virginia with Robb and Wilder on stage; Wilder pledged his endorsement of Robb, and they all shook hands. The feud was over, and hope was breaking out all over.

Finally, North was under attack on national television by prominent Republicans who had worked for President Reagan. The most damning attack came from Nancy Reagan. When asked during an interview with PBS if her husband would endorse Oliver North, she said, "I know Ollie North has a great deal of trouble separating fact from fantasy. He lied to my husband and lied about my husband ... and that's about what I think of Oliver North."

Ron called to say that Ed Rollins, Reagan's former campaign manager and my husband's former partner, had given him a heads-up about the Nancy Reagan interview. David Doak, Robb's longtime adviser and media consultant, had an ad cut from the clip with Mrs. Reagan and ready to go by the next day. We continued to run with that spot, pointing directly at North's inability to tell the truth. The negative comments only emboldened his more ardent supporters to do more.

We were heading into the last ten days of the campaign, and we needed a rip-roaring closing speech that would complement our paid media hammering home all North's lies, misdeeds, and misinformation we had been stressing for months. I called our press secretaries, Peggy Wilhide and Bert Rohrer, and our researcher, Cara Brown, into my office to discuss what we needed to do. After much discussion, Peggy said she understood what I wanted: we would use as a template a speech made by Alabama Senator Howell Heflin some years earlier. The speech would be written in an almost singsong style, synthesizing all we had said about North over the last year. After days of writing, rewriting, and polishing, we showed it to the senator, and he loved it, as did Lynda. Before he left on the final tour around the state, he promised me he would deliver the speech word for word, and he did just that. It began, "Let me tell you something about my opponent," and continued, "my opponent is a document-shredding, Constitution-trashing ... ," concluding with "who can't tell the difference between the truth and a lie."

The crowds at the first stop in Roanoke, Virginia, erupted in cheers. This is what they were waiting for. Word spread, and at each subsequent stop, with Governor Wilder alongside

Robbs, the crowds grew. By the final stop, the crowd was repeating parts of the speech.

By the end of the weekend before election day, Geoff Garin, the best pollster I ever met, had conducted a rolling tracking poll. When he called with the results, he said all movement was in our direction, and while he wouldn't tell me we would win, he did say he was feeling confident in his numbers.

Election Day was November 8, and it was also Ron's and my fifteenth wedding anniversary. Everyone was out at polling stations, making phone calls to voters and giving rides to the polls. I had sent Ron to Hampton Roads two weeks prior to work with Congressman Bobby Scott on African American Get Out the Vote operations, and by midday he would drive back to Northern Virginia to be with me for the results. During the day, I remember feeling as if I was trying to move a mountain. I sneaked away from the office for an hour to meet Ron at home. Senator Robb was very sweet and understanding that I was gone for a little while, and when he called the office with a question, he told the staff not to bother me but to see if they could get him an answer.

Finally, the polls closed, and by early election night, the election was called by several networks. We had beat the odds and Oliver North by three percentage points. The victory party was one of the largest I have ever seen, apart from a presidential one, with over one hundred members of the media from around the world covering the results and victory party live. When it was clear we would be the winner, and after receiving a concession call from North, Robb, alongside his family, made his way through the halls of the hotel, through the kitchen and backstage to greet all the supporters. When the Robb family entered the stage, the crowd erupted as he approached the microphone to say what had become a tradition after each of his winning campaigns: "How sweet it is," and it certainly was. When Senator Robb called me to join him on stage, I was reluctant. I was on the ballroom floor with Ron and surrounded by hundreds of supporters. I didn't want to leave him, but at his encouragement, I joined the family and revelers on stage and soaked it all in. I have never again felt such great satisfaction as I did that night.

After our victory over Lt. Col. Oliver North, I received the "Pollie Award," voted by my national peers at the American Association of Political Consultants for "Campaign Manager of the Year 1994." This was a pretty big deal for anyone's career, let alone someone who had just run her first statewide campaign and won. The other person to receive it was Newt Gingrich for his Contract with America and winning a Republican majority in the House of Representatives. With Ron by my side, I walked to the stage to accept the award in a ballroom filled with political workers and consultants from across the country.

R. J. Cutler's film *A Perfect Candidate* came out in 1995. The title did not refer to my candidate; it focused more on Oliver North, the charismatic candidate. While it did not present my candidate in the most flattering light, it did do a good job of depicting the campaigns. Senator Robb asked me to screen the film, and I did. I watched it at home, with no one else in the room. I wouldn't let Ron watch it with me because I needed to focus only on the screen and didn't know what to expect. When the movie concluded, I felt the tears running down my face. I was still amazed at the intensity and media attention the campaign had garnered; amazed, too, that against so many odds we were able to pull off a win. When Ron saw me, he asked what was wrong. I told him I couldn't believe all we had gone through: the land mines we had dodged, and the obstacles we'd overcome. We were successful, and I was proud of myself. After watching all the scenes in the film of North and his team of bragging, chest-thumping men who assured themselves they would win, I was overwhelmed that Senator Robb and our team led by me as campaign manager had whooped 'em good. Ron hugged me hard and told me how proud he was of me. That was the best feeling in the world.

In 2006, I found a description of our campaign in the book *Mudslingers: The Top 25 Negative Political Campaigns of All Time* by Kerwin C. Swint, professor of political science and former campaign consultant and political commentator. Our campaign was listed at Number 12, and I would be described as a well-known Democratic Party operative in Virginia—that was news to me! I never viewed our campaign as negative, since everything we said and advertised was documented fact, and it was enough to convince voters to vote for my candidate—and that's what campaigns are all about.

Having a supportive husband during the tumultuous and highly publicized time of the Robb for Senate campaign in 1994 was critical to my ability to be as strong, focused, and resolute in my job as campaign manager. He was always there to support me. Even though Ron was much more experienced and knowledgeable on political history and campaigns, he never once offered unsolicited advice. And he was circumspect when I did seek it.

# 7

## Ridin' with Biden

My job as Charles Robb's campaign manager taught me that this work was perfect for me: I enjoyed organizing, planning strategies, working collectively with others toward shared policy positions, traveling, and meeting interesting people. I enjoyed making a difference, and I was pretty good at it. Ron understood campaigns, and he encouraged me. He had made a living running campaigns when he was younger and understood why I loved it.

It was the beginning of the holiday season in 1994, and I was shutting down Senator Robb's against-the-odds reelection, but that win was not enough for the Democrats to maintain their majority in the US Senate. So, while we were celebrating, many other Democrats were not. I wasn't sure what I wanted to do next, but I knew I wasn't finished with managing campaigns. I had held a few jobs in several congressional offices before working in campaigns and had enjoyed them. But once I had the taste of the excitement and comradery and sense of purpose that goes with most campaigns, I didn't think there was any going back

There is always a period of jubilation and pride after managing a winning campaign. After the jubilation, there is a let-down period of missing all the activity and comradery that makes a great campaign. Ron never pushed me in any direction for my next job. I told him I wanted to run another campaign, but there was not going to be another statewide campaign in Virginia until 1997, and I wasn't prepared to go to another state to run a campaign. So, I thought about doing political campaign consulting, but I didn't feel comfortable about broad marketing.

A few weeks after the close of Senator Robb's campaign, I got a call from Tim Ridley, who had been chief of staff, or administrative assistant (AA) as they were called then, for New Jersey Senator Frank Lautenberg and former presidential staff for Biden for President in 1988. Senator Biden's longtime AA had just retired, and he was looking to hire someone to take the job. Tim wanted me to meet with Biden. I told Tim I wasn't done with campaigns yet, but Ron, who knew more about campaign life than I did, told me he thought it would be a smart move to pursue the opportunity. He reminded me that I had met Biden in Miami in 1980 at a Biden for Senate fundraiser we hosted at our home. So, although I was more than a little intimidated with the prospects of this potential new job, I told Tim I would meet with Biden.

January 1995 was a time of transition for both Senator Biden and me. Congressman Newt Gingrich's Contract with America had helped Republicans win control of the House of Representatives for the first time in nearly fifty years, a net gain of fifty-four seats; in addition, for the first time in ten years, Republicans held a majority in the Senate. Biden was no longer chairman of the Judiciary Committee, and Democrats were in a funk.

Biden's longtime aide and AA, Ted Kaufman, retired after more than twenty years on Biden's staff. Ted would usually join Biden on the daily train commutes from Wilmington to DC and back. Biden was going to miss that rapport he shared with Ted, his trusted staffer, political adviser, and friend. After a few weeks of back-and-forth discussions, Biden offered me the job as his new chief of staff, and I accepted. Biden later told me he hired me because in Robb's race for reelection, the highest-profile race in the country, I didn't make one political mistake ... at least none that the press wrote about or that negatively impacted the campaign. So, with my aide-de-camp Bryson alongside me, we went to the Hill.

It was a time when comity between the two parties was fraying. The Democrats who had held chairmanships of their congressional committees were no longer in charge. The Moral Majority had mobilized conservative Christians for the past ten years, and Newt Gingrich's Contract with America continued that mission for Republicans. Newly elected Republican members were emboldened by their victories.

Although Senator Biden was now a ranking member, not chairman, of the Senate Judiciary Committee, he no longer controlled what legislation would be moved through the committee. And his opponent in his bid for reelection in 1996 owned several Christian radio stations. In the previous Congress, Biden had worked to pass the Omnibus Crime Bill that would ban assault weapons. Now Democrats couldn't pass anything.

Life in the Senate was very different from that on the campaign trail, and Biden and Robb were quite different personalities. To begin with, my days weren't nearly as frenetic as they had been during the campaign. And Biden was a different boss. Senator Robb ran his office and his campaign in a military style: if you were in charge, you were in charge, and the hierarchy flowed down. Biden's style was much more freewheeling. And as everyone worked to adjust to the new political reality, Biden continued to ride the train daily to and from Delaware. I liked and had great respect for him, as a person and senator—how could you not admire him if you knew the story of his losing his wife and daughter in a car wreck before Christmas and before being sworn in as the newly elected US Senator from Delaware?

In my effort to try to understand what he most needed from me, I would occasionally ride the train with him to Delaware after the last senate vote of the day, working through some of his ideas as he traveled home, then taking the train back to DC and my home that same evening. Truth was, though, he was always his own best political adviser.

Biden and his sister, Valerie, were planning the upcoming reelection campaign, something they had done together since he was elected in 1972. Most of his staff in Delaware had been with him since the beginning, including during his presidential bids, and they knew his rhythm and that of the state of Delaware. I would offer advice and suggestions, but I was finding it frustrating to be on the outside of the political campaign. He was as good a politician as I had ever seen, and he and Val and his team were setting him up again for another big win. Meanwhile, I was meeting regularly with staff on specific legislative and political issues and making sure the staff had the help they needed to get their jobs done for Biden and Delaware. I knew I had been given a great opportunity, but I also knew I was not done running campaigns.

During the fall of 1996, before the November election, I was contacted by Don Beyer, then Virginia's lieutenant governor. Beyer was planning to run for governor in 1997, and since my 1994 race had been successful in Virginia, he wanted me to run his governor's race. Election night 1996 arrived, and Biden won with 60 percent of the vote. I told him I wanted to get back to running campaigns and that I had accepted Beyer's offer of the job of campaign manager. I was going back to Virginia politics.

Those two years with Biden were a lot more normal than the previous two, when I was running Robb's campaign. Working for Biden, I was only out of the office when I took the train with Biden to Delaware. Around this time, Ron's younger son, Brent, enrolled at George Mason Law School and came to live with us. We had a bedroom on the lower level of our home with its own bath where he could have a private space. Ron's father needed carotid artery surgery, and he would also move in with us after that surgery. We had a full house, dogs included, but we were all happy it seemed. Ron's dad liked to cook, and he often made dinners for us during the week when I was sometimes with Biden later in the evening and Ron was attending many fundraising receptions. It worked well for a while.

When we were home on the weekends, Ron would spend time with his dad watching Yankees baseball or Washington Redskins or Oklahoma Sooners football, sometimes with their eyes closed, snoring away. This time helped Ron and his dad deepen their relationship as they discussed choices each had made regarding family when they were younger. Ron's dad admitted it was a mistake to let Ron's mother handle his day-to-day discipline and upbringing.

I enjoyed cooking on the weekends, and Brent would come and go with his studies and dates. We had an easy, relaxed home life.

After I left Biden's staff, I had little interaction with him until 2004, when my brother and his wife were trying to adopt a second child from a Catholic adoption agency in Vietnam. Their first child, a girl from the same agency, was such a gift to them, and they desperately wanted a sister for her to complete their family. They chose Vietnam because after a lot of research they appreciated the culture and the way Vietnamese children were revered. At the time of the second adoption request, several years later, no adoptions were allowed to Americans due to reports of corrupt adoption procedures and horror stories about mistreated children and child trafficking in countries like Vietnam. Intercountry adoptions were complicated to begin with because of the need to adhere to the laws of three separate jurisdictions: those of the sending country, US federal immigration law, and individual state laws and regulations.

The first hurdle was getting the Vietnamese to agree to allow this specific adoption. Jan Scruggs, founder of the Vietnam Veterans Wall and a friend of mine, arranged a meeting for me with a high-level Vietnamese government official who was in Washington visiting with Jan and other members of the Wall board of directors. When I explained the circumstances to this official, he made a commitment to me (and my brother via a phone call) that the Vietnamese government would allow his adoption to go through. The first hurdle cleared, we now had to get the US government on board.

We scheduled several meetings with my brother and his wife and daughter, enlisting help from various members of the US Senate; the most important participant would be Senator Biden. Biden, majority leader Harry Reid, and Senator Mary Landrieu (a member of the adoption caucus) all agreed to help. It was decided my brother and his wife should go ahead with the adoption process and travel to Vietnam. The procedure through the Vietnamese government was expedited, and they left the Vietnamese government offices with approval in hand. Now was the hard part. When they were received at the US Consulate in Hanoi, their application to travel with their new daughter was denied. After a frantic call from my brother, the groundwork and plans we had laid months prior with the senators were about to be set into motion. Senators Reid and Landrieu's staffs called the US State Department, alerting them of the situation. But what made the difference was communication from Senator Biden directly to Secretary of State Colin Powell. My brother returned to our consulate the next day and was told his situation was being handled at the highest levels of our government and that he should return the next day with possible news. The next evening, my brother and sister-in-law and their new daughter received approval from the US government and were driven to the airport with the appropriate documents, approved by the United States. I'll never forget what Biden did for our family that day. No one should be surprised, though, as anyone who knows Biden would tell you, he would move heaven and earth to unite a family.

# 8

# Finding My Voice

T he political climate had shifted in 1997, and while Don Beyer was a popular lieutenant governor, getting elected as governor was going to be a different story. Governors in Virginia can only serve one four-year term, and the current governor was a Republican, the affable son of winning Redskin coach George Allen. Beyer was a businessman, the owner of a car dealership, and people liked that. He would run against Jim Gilmore, a hard-nosed Republican attorney from the Richmond area.

Don was smart, easygoing, and well-liked, and we were raising one heck of a lot of money. Since Don was such a well-liked candidate and lieutenant governor, the campaign capitalized on those things during the spring, since we were mainly dealing with personalities rather than policy at that point. By contrast, Don's opponent, Jim Gilmore, looked like a sourpuss all the time and was not a particularly likeable individual.

In early summer, Geoff Garin, our trusted pollster, held a focus group in Virginia Beach during which the issue of the car tax came up. The car tax was an annual personal property tax on vehicles assessed by the county in which the car is housed; the amount of tax was based on that year's assessed value. In some larger, wealthier counties, that tax could top $2,000 per car. People hated the tax, which they were required to pay every year, but it helped prop up local governments. People in Hampton Roads paid the tax in the summer. For the rest of the state, particularly northern Virginia's Fairfax County, the largest county in the state, where Democrats needed to bring in a big win to win the state, the tax was due right before Election Day.

Some campaigns I won and some campaigns I lost. This one for governor of Virginia we lost BIG. Local governments objected to removing the car tax; the lost revenue couldn't be made up in other ways. And Beyer didn't want to lose that income, as he had proposed major increases in education spending. From a political perspective, you were a winner if you were for ending the tax. If you wanted to keep the tax, you did so at your own peril. The Republican candidates embraced the dishonest "No Car Tax" pledge. We tried to get Beyer to agree to some plan to end the tax. We tried every equation we could, but we just couldn't find a way to make the numbers add up and pay for new education spending. A few advisers outside the campaign tried to tell Beyer that a promise to spend money on education could negate the potency of "no car tax." Of course, they were wrong, but the candidate wanted to believe those advisers. As the summer was coming to an end, the poll numbers began slipping, and infighting began between other candidates on the ticket and in the House of Delegates, as they began to smell possible defeat.

Staffers hired to work the coordinate campaign to elect the Democratic statewide ticket and get out the vote believed statewide campaign managers should meet to try to stop negative commentary about Beyer. I couldn't tell them why Beyer wouldn't embrace the only issue of that campaign season. At some point, they insulted me and my candidate enough that I let loose with several expletives, only to read about my reaction in the *Richmond Times-Dispatch* and the *Washington Post* in the next few days. I was angry, and Ron saw it for what it was, sexism, and he was more incensed about it at that point than I was. I just needed to deal with any fallout. I could not believe my swearing made for a story in *The Washington Post*. I offered to resign, but Beyer didn't accept my resignation. I even got a call from friends at the Clinton White House asking if they could help. This was not the first time in my career I felt sexism directed at me, but it was the most embarrassing. Little did I know this would set me up on my path for my next twenty-year journey.

Election Day was a huge, complete loss for all Democratic statewide candidates; Democrats barely maintained control of the House of Delegates. We were decimated. When your candidate wins an election, it is their win. When your candidate loses, the manager is to blame. So, with this loss, I stopped managing campaigns and began in a new direction.

# 9

## Out of the Frying Pan and into the Fire

The summer before Beyer's disastrous loss, we suffered a personal loss. Ron's dad, Hook, had been living with us since his carotid artery surgery, and on June 13, his daytime caretaker called to say Hook had become gravely ill and was being transported to the hospital. I had been living part time in Richmond for the campaign but came home as soon as Ron called. At just around midnight, we got a call from the hospital telling us to hurry if we wanted to say goodbye. Ron, Brent, and I hurried to the hospital, but we were too late. Ron stayed at his dad's bedside for a time, then made some arrangements with the hospital. When he got home, he said, "Now I'm an orphan."

Several days later, we transported Hook's body to Ada, Oklahoma, so that he could be buried beside his wife.

After the governor's race in 1997, I needed to move on to the next step of my career. While I enjoyed so much of campaign life, I wanted to find something I enjoyed that involved less travel, where I could enjoy our upper-middle-class home in the bucolic village of Great Falls. Upon making this move, we had stopped hosting weekly fundraisers in our home and began enjoying the quieter and slower style of suburban living. It was our little heaven where we had room to breathe and relax.

Not long after Election Day, a friend of mine who I had worked with in a congressional office called to ask if I would be interested in managing their nationwide grassroots effort to defeat a piece of legislation. It was perfect timing for me and would begin my new career in grassroots organizing and federal lobbying. I was working part time out of our home and part time out of an office in DC.

During this period, Brent was still going to law school, but I noticed that he never seemed to leave at the same times or return home at normal times. He always had his gym bag with him and never talked about his studies or school. I told Ron that I thought something was off and asked him to talk to Brent. He told me he was sure I was just reading too much into his coming and goings, so I dropped it.

Memorial Day weekend arrived, and Ron and I were planning to barbecue ribs and go to the movies. On Sunday night, we asked Brent if he wanted to go to the movies with us. He told us he had plans for the night, so we went without him. He didn't come home that night and didn't call, but we weren't too concerned about it, even though he usually told us if he would not be home. Later in the day, we started to grow concerned that we hadn't heard from him. He knew we were planning dinner, and he had never said he wouldn't be home. He was now twenty-one years old, but he was still living with us, and all we asked was he communicate with us on when he would be home.

When he didn't return the next night and hadn't called, we were very concerned. Ron went into Brent's bedroom and found he had cleaned out his closet: clothes and shoes were gone, and only his law school books were left behind. Eventually Ron called his ex-wife to ask if she had heard from him. She told him she had no idea what we had done, but he would now be living with her instead of with us. Ron was shocked and beside himself. The last time we had spoken to Brent, everything had been fine. We had no arguments with him, nor had we placed any demands on him. We stuck by our word of not interfering with his activities while he lived with us and attended law school. We paid his tuition and gave him Ron's old Cadillac; in return, we expected him to study hard in school. We were completely befuddled as to what had happened. We concluded that something was going on that we weren't aware of; we hoped he would eventually talk to us about any issues he was having.

My heart ached for my husband; he had always tried to help and encourage and support Brent in whatever he wanted to do, and I was right there with him. Neither Ron nor I had argued with Brent; we always tried to include him with what we were doing and did not believe we pressured him in any way except to do his best. As the months went by, we would rarely talk about Brent, but he was on both of our minds.

Around Christmas in 1998, Ron took a drive to his ex-wife's house and knocked on the door. Brent talked to him briefly, and they decided they would talk more after the holidays. Brent never discussed any of this with me, but within the next several months Ron and Brent did meet and talk. Brent finally confessed to Ron he had not been attending law school and with the time for graduation approaching, he had panicked and left. He told his mother he was having problems with us and had to leave. His mother's husband told Brent if was going to stay there he had to contribute, so he helped get Brent a job in a warehouse stacking boxes. Brent made Ron promise never to tell his mother what he had done, that he would never graduate and become a lawyer. It was an incredibly sad situation. Ron questioned himself about not seeing any signs of Brent's deception. He questioned his parenting abilities and worried about why his son could not confess to him that he was not going to school. I felt helpless, as all I could do was assure Ron he hadn't done anything wrong to his son. Over the next few months, Ron worked to encourage Brent to open up emotionally and even suggested he seek help with a therapist. It would take time before Brent was comfortable coming to our house, and we never spoke of it again.

In addition to Ron's and my regular work schedules, we both took time off during the fall to volunteer for senate campaigns in other states. We generally volunteered for two to three weeks at the end of a campaign, so we got our fill of excitement while raising our stature among those we helped. We always went to a state where a race was tight, and we could make a difference and be appreciated. Ron went to Nevada in 1998 to help Senator Harry Reid, who won reelection by only 428 votes, and I went to South Carolina to help Senator Fritz Hollings win a tight race.

My involvement in Senator Hollings's campaign had been part of a grassroots effort to enlist the support of a broad group of consumers and businesses. The largest of the corporations, a Fortune 100 American company, was impressed with my skills and signed me to a yearly contract for legislative strategy and lobbying. So, I became a self-employed legislative and political consultant, and I worked for that company for the next twenty years.

At some point during my first year working with them, when sitting at a large conference table with other consultants and corporate execs, I realized I was the only woman. There were more than twenty suits in attendance and me. I thought about being a woman in the business of politics—or any business for that matter—but politics was not as hard a business for women to break into because women were such an integral part of campaigns—even though, for most, it was volunteer jobs or arranging events. Politics and campaigns were filled with women, but that was not the case in corporate America. I began to consider how hard it was for women to join the men's corporate club. I had been lucky to hold top leadership roles in campaigns and on the Hill, but being the only woman in this corporate room smacked me right in the face. I recognized this was something that needed to change, and I would later work for that change.

# 10

## The New Millenium
### *A Time of Pain*

In January 2000, Ron and I began a new year and a new century with an adventure. We were asked by the Gore for President campaign to spend several weeks in New Hampshire trying to combat the insurgent campaign of Senator Bill Bradley. New Hampshire held the first primary in the nation, and Gore needed a big victory. Bradley was trying to find some momentum with the liberals in the seacoast towns, so that is where we were stationed. It was the first time we had worked together on a presidential campaign and the first time either of us had worked in New Hampshire.

We had fun together! We stayed at a hotel on the beach in Seabrook, where the ten-degree wind would blow off the beach directly through our sliding glass doors from the balcony overlooking the beach and the frozen waves, but we did not care. We were together, doing something we both loved, away from Washington, in snow piled high. Ron, who hated the cold, did not complain, as there was a lot of snuggling going on. We did our organizing work in between visits to Widow Fletcher's, a bar that served the best New England clam chowder. We bought winter weather gear as we traveled around and even stood together in the snow and cold holding Gore for President signs when CBS's Dan Rather needed a shot for the television news. In between calls with clients, we laughed, worked, and got to know New Hampshirites, and we loved every minute of it. And when Gore won New Hampshire, we rejoiced and left satisfied, ready to go back to DC.

As usual, we planned a trip to St. Martin after the election, only this time, the election results were not known. It was agonizing waiting for the counting of the chads, and then the Supreme Court decision, ending with Gore conceding the election to George W. Bush. Our high hopes for the new millennium ended with shock—and the following year would be worse.

On the morning of September 11, 2001, I was getting ready to go to DC for a 10 a.m. client meeting, when news broke that two planes had hit the World Trade Center buildings. It was hard to compute what was happening. We knew what we saw was real, but we never imagined an attack like that would happen on our own soil. So, listening to the news reports on the radio, I began my drive into the city for my meeting. As I was crossing the bridge into DC, I heard the report that the Pentagon had been hit by another plane, and looking across the Potomac River, I could see the smoke billowing in the sky. On autopilot, I continued driving. My meeting was to be held several blocks from the White House, and eventually we heard the meeting was cancelled and the government was telling people to go home. Traffic was a nightmare, and the cell phone lines were jammed with frantic callers trying to reach their loved ones. I finally got through to Ron at his office, one block from the White House, and he said he was going to wait a while for the traffic to disperse. Within minutes of trying to drive through the traffic back to Virginia, fighter planes flew over us in the city and military tanks were driving through the streets. It was like the movie *Independence Day* where the city was attacked, and we were living it.

Eventually I made my way home, and several hours later so did Ron. My parents, who were still living in Winchester, called and told us to go out to their place to be farther away from the city in case there were more attacks. Ron would not hear of leaving our home unless it was necessary. We watched the reports, glued to the television all afternoon.

Ron insisted on going to work the next day, saying those terrorists were not going to intimidate him. Now cars parked in garages near the White House and other government buildings would be screened by security, and the government would establish a new agency, Homeland Security, to coordinate intelligence and security across the wider government agencies. Airports would have security check points, and everyone needed to go through magnetometers searching for explosive devices or guns or knives. Our lives as Americans changed forever, as we were faced with the reality that we were much less secure than we previously believed.

By this time, twenty years into our marriage, we began to realize we were much happier at home together than going to parties and other social events. Often, when we were out, we exchanged the look that asked, "can we go home now?" We rarely asked other couples to join us on holidays, but we enjoyed spending time with two couples who were close friends.

The day before Thanksgiving in 2004, we were sitting in our family room with my family, who had driven from Pennsylvania to have Thanksgiving dinner at our house, watching a football game. We had a big house, so no one had to spend the night in a hotel, and our large dining table could seat all twelve of us.

The phone rang, and it was Patrick, Karen's husband. Karen and their two children, Kristin and Stephen, had been in a bad car accident. Stephen had been taken by helicopter to Children's Hospital, while Kristin was taken to the local hospital for treatment of her injuries and to be checked out for further injuries. Karen had not been injured. Ron flew to Miami, where they were all living, but before leaving told me to find the life insurance policy he had taken on Stephen. At this time, there was serious question on whether Stephen would survive his injuries.

The next day, Thanksgiving, Ron became aware of Karen's drinking problem. Her drinking had become a problem in the late nineties, but we knew nothing about it. Living in Miami made it easy for Karen to hide her problem from us, and her children were admonished not to say anything during their summer visits. Karen had been taking the kids on a camping trip for Thanksgiving and was driving drunk; neither of the children were wearing seat belts. Stephen had been thrown from the car, and Kristin had severe lacerations on her legs. Days later, after Stephen had been stabilized and finally regained consciousness, he was moved back to a hospital closer to their home. He would remain in the hospital for a month and then to a rehabilitation facility to restore full movement to one side of his body. Thankfully, since he was still a young boy, his brain would be able to heal from the trauma over the next months.

Ron called me every day with updates on Stephen until he regained consciousness. Once he seemed to be recovering, Ron asked me to fly to Miami and help him convince Karen to go into a treatment facility for alcoholics. Karen and I never fought, and I always tried to tread lightly when it came to giving her advice—I usually left that up to her father—but this was different. I decided early on that, since we were not that different in age, I could not function as her mother, but I was not her friend either. I tried to emulate my stepmother in dealing with Karen, but she consistently turned to her father if she wanted to talk about anything beyond what she felt comfortable discussing with me. It seemed to be a workable relationship. In some ways, I put on blinders when it came to dealing with Ron's children, and Ron did too as it pertained to Karen and her insecurities.

We had absolutely no idea how to manage confronting her. Neither Ron nor I had ever dealt with anything like this. We both called around to alcohol addiction facilities and received guidance on how best to approach her. I had also made inquiries into a facility in Maryland to see if they had availability, as we thought it would be best to remove her from her current surroundings. Once we did that, Ron went with Karen to her house to get clothes and toiletries. Karen wouldn't allow me to go, as she said the house was a mess. Ron told me her house was in shambles, cat urine and feces everywhere, as well as clothes and old food and wine bottles. We couldn't imagine what the children had been going through.

Ron and I sat with Karen and her teenage daughter, Kristin, who had also been with her in the accident. We told Karen she needed help, not only for herself but for her children. I remember her strong resistance, of course, but we continued talking with her until she finally agreed to check herself in to the facility. Ron had to be in Michigan on business, so Kristin and I flew back to Virginia with Karen. When I think back to this, part of the reason Ron was not with us was because he could not cope with the situation. He was an extraordinarily strong man, but the seriousness of this event hurt him to his core. He blamed himself for Karen's troubles due to his divorce from her mother. We had a day or so to wait until the facility could take her, and I discovered Karen was hiding liquor in her bedroom. I did not call her out on this, as I had been warned if we kept liquor from her, she could have a seizure. Kristin and I drove her to the facility, where we were given the rules on contact and visits. We left hoping they would be able to help her.

She was in that facility for almost forty-five days. She came out with a good attitude, and we hoped that would last. We put her on a plane back to Miami a few days later with plenty of promises to let us know if she needed help. Our hopes were diminished when I went to the bedroom where Karen was staying to change the sheets and discovered she had been drinking vanilla extract and mouthwash during her brief time at our home before she returned to Miami. I learned later that this behavior was common with alcoholics when they could not get their drink of choice. So much for the treatment program. We were emotionally devastated.

Things for Karen would never get better, but life for the children was getting worse. Eventually, we told Karen's husband, Patrick, if he didn't remove the kids from her house, we would go to court and take custody. Patrick had moved out and sometime later took the children with him. The court granted Patrick custody of the children in their divorce. To say we were relieved would be an understatement.

We would continue to send Karen to various treatment centers and facilities, in various parts of the country and in Miami. Unfortunately, none of the treatments worked, so eventually, after a lot of money and heartache, we gave up. We finally took away the car we had leased for her, and she and her ex-husband lost the house to bankruptcy court. Ron set her up in an apartment near a bus line and the metro, and we paid all her living expenses, medical treatments, and anything else she needed. I had no idea no idea the amount of money Ron was spending on her, but I knew after so many years it had to be adding up. Not only had it drained Ron emotionally, but I would also find out much later it nearly drained our retirement funds. Karen met another addict, Morris, in one of the facilities we sent her to, and they began living together, so we paid the living expenses for both of them. Somehow, we learned to accept this, periodically receiving calls from Morris when Karen would be taken by ambulance to the hospital for alcohol-related seizures or for treatment of infections. At least there was someone there to make sure she received medical treatment. This would continue until August 2015, ten years later.

# 11

## Women Awaken

It was the spring of 2008; the presidential primary season had begun, and it was a fight between Senators Hillary Clinton and Barack Obama. I supported Hillary, and Ron backed Obama. We didn't do this by design; it was just the way we both felt. I had gradually become more engaged in activist activities in support of women and believed it was time we had a qualified woman president. But there was no question Barack Obama was an incredibly talented, charismatic, groundbreaking candidate as well.

While attending a Virginia Women's Democratic Party breakfast in Richmond in the late spring of that year, I said out loud that I was tired of women being pushed aside. I turned to former Virginia Attorney General Mary Sue Terry, at the time the only woman ever elected statewide in Virginia, and stated that we needed to do something about that. Mary Sue had receded from political involvement after losing the governor's race in 1993, but she agreed it was time to reengage in this kind of venture.

We talked a lot during July about what we could do and how we could do it. We decided to hold an organizing event on September 23 at Mary Sue's family cattle farm in Critz, Virginia. We invited over one hundred women: Democratic Party activists, elected officials, campaign workers, and community activists. Twenty-three women attended from Roanoke, Arlington, Virginia Beach, Abingdon, Winchester, Martinsville, Richmond, and more. We slept on the floor, the couch, and the chairs. I slept on the floor beside Mary Sue's German shepherd.

That weekend, we planned and plotted, and "The Farm Team" was created. The role of The Farm Team was to train and assist women less experienced in political campaigns in how to run and win elections across Virginia. A simple mission! There were quite a few jabs about our name, but we believed what mattered most was what we could accomplish.

We made a big splash in Virginia political circles and beyond. We received great press about our political potential from local and state newspapers and television and even a few national blogs; Mary Sue's reengagement gave us visibility. A few women's organizations for similar purposes had started out of Richmond, but they hadn't lasted more than six months. The organizations that failed were local to Richmond with Richmond women as members. Most of them were more a social organization for woman, either not active on the local party committees or having minimal experience in campaigns. The question was: would this one be long-lasting and make an impact?

We organized by region and appointed women to head up recruitment in their region. We asked all women,

women who were members of the PTA or other local organizations, not just the Democratic Party, to contact us if
they heard of women candidates who needed help planning a campaign, and they enthusiastically called. Several
of us took to the road to spend a day or two with each candidate, helping them frame a message, develop their stump
speech, raise money, and organize a campaign. We helped a
young, single lawyer with young children successfully run
for commonwealth attorney and helped an African American woman get elected to the town council, becoming the
youngest woman ever elected in Virginia. A mayor in the
town of Lynchburg was running for reelection, but Jerry
Falwell Jr. of Liberty University, whose father founded the
Moral Majority and Liberty University, was fighting against
her and openly promoting her opponent. Falwell had taped
a conversation with her and altered the recording to dis-
tort a statement she made, then shared it with the local
newspaper. Many local politicians and businesses who supported her did not want to engage publicly against Falwell,
as the university was a large employer in the city, and fac-
ulty and staff frequented their businesses. She called us for
help. We drafted a press release with a copy of an op-ed
I wrote attacking Falwell as being underhanded and un-
Christian and challenging the newspaper to print it. They
did, but the local politicians were apoplectic. They called
the mayor and me, saying this was going to cost all of them
their reelection, but we stood our ground. One thing we
would not do was be intimidated by bullies. I drove four
hours to Lynchburg for Election Day and stood with the
mayor. Not only did she win with the largest vote ever, but
all the other Democrats on the city council also won their
races. That was a good day, and we proved our worth and
our political savvy.

When we organized The Farm Team, women comprised only 11 percent of the general assembly, one of the lowest participation rates in the country. As we grew, we began helping more and more women run, and more were winning. It was fulfilling to motivate more politically inexperienced women to learn the process and best practices to win elections. We were collectively developing a new purpose. Of course, we experienced the usual dismissal by the local men. Case in point was a meeting I attended with several politically experienced local men. The purpose of the meeting was to discuss the campaign of a young woman running for city council. We discussed strategy and ideas to help her become known. I later learned that after I left the meeting with an understanding the ideas we discussed would be implemented, the men told her if she listened to me and not them, they would abandon her. She ignored them. It was going to be a challenge for her to win that race, but she ran a strong race and held her head high.

Our first big move came when a delegate seat opened in northern Virginia. This happened only one day before our official kick-off of women in December 2008, when the current delegate resigned his seat. We couldn't think of a better location for this event than at the home of Senator Charles and Lynda Johnson Robb overlooking the Potomac River in McLean. They didn't often open their home to larger crowds except on special occasions, but it was the perfect venue, with loads of room around the indoor pool and plenty of tables for seating in the three-sided glass-walled room overlooking the river below. Senator Robb scurried around taking photos and acted as official greeter. Lynda welcomed everyone and acted as our major cheerleader. She had seen so much and lived through so much during her father's presidency and then her husband's campaigns. All the women there paid close attention to her anecdotes, memories, and best practices. It helped that she had three girls of her own and reminded all of us how far women had come and how much further we could go. When asked, I remember telling Senator Robb that maybe fifty women would show up on a Sunday afternoon. Two hundred women showed up.

Lynda Robb spoke about women's history and rights, and many others chimed in. I then stood and asked who was considering running for elective office. Several women stood up, but one woman stood and spoke. She said she was going to run for the seat of delegate Brian Moran, who had stepped down a week before to run for governor. Only a handful of women knew her. She told us her name was Charnielle Herring, and she was going to run and win. We were all impressed with her pitch, courage, and boldness. She was a young African American lawyer, raised by her single mother, who also volunteered for SALT (Service and Love Together, a service to help the homeless), and had experienced homelessness herself as a young child. She had a great life story and was clearly smart, determined, and fearless. This was the kind of woman we needed!

The political powers that be at the time—the men— decided that the seat should go to the mayor of Alexandria, and they didn't want to hear about anyone else. We organized a quiet pressure campaign carried out by women state senators, women delegates, and other prominent Democratic women calling the men directly, telling them to back off, that we had a qualified woman of color we wanted to run for that seat. And back off they eventually did. We helped her form a candidate committee, knocked on doors, and contributed the first $1,000 toward the campaign. She won that race and several more thereafter.

She went on to become the first African America woman to be elected chair of the Democratic Party of Virginia, and then several years later, she was elected by her caucus to be majority leader in the Virginia House of Delegates. The idea I had with Mary Sue Terry was taking hold, and things were changing.

By 2011, more and more women were running for positions at all levels of government in Virginia, and it became too much for the few of us to help them all. At this time, I was contacted by another group, Emerge. Emerge was founded by a group of women in California, and their mission was to recruit, train, and provide a network for Democratic women who wanted to run for office. At that point, twelve other states had Emerge organizations, and they wanted us to become number thirteen. We had the same purpose and similar training classes. Emerge provided a seventy-hour training program format, and they managed the website and the day-to-day operations in addition to the training, which took a big load off my shoulders. It took some convincing, but ultimately, I convinced our other board members to support the move, and The Farm Team merged with Emerge to form EmergeVA.

I was tired and ready for a break. In addition to my work with clients, I spent many hours and a good bit of money for the cause, and I was looking for someone to help lead the new effort. At that time, women comprised over 15 percent of the legislature, an increase but not enough. So, after the first year's successes, I turned over the reins to a new leadership team. I can't say it was easy, and in many ways I regretted turning over the reins to the person I did. Yes, she was experienced and had held elective office several times herself, but she was becoming abrasive, and that was not how I operated. But I was done worrying about it, and together with her team, she made great progress with the program for the next several years. As of this writing, women comprise 32 percent of the Virginia General Assembly. We have elected three Democratic women to the US Congress, all EmergeVA grads. I am proud of the impact of these two organizations, which I founded, across Virginia.

# 12

## The Business of Lobbying

Google defines lobbying as "an organized attempt by members of the public to influence politicians or public officials on a particular issue." When Ron was asked by our granddaughter what lobbying was, he described it as "long hours of boredom punctuated by moments of sheer terror." I had heard Ron's description before in other contexts, and in researching the phrase, I found it may have originated in the First World War to describe trench warfare on the western front; some references also say that pilots in the First World War used the phrase to describe their jobs. No one seems to know its exact origin, but it's a perfect description of the business of lobbying.

The business of politics is both ever-changing and always consistent. There are always going to be elected officials who hold the purse strings and always people trying to spend the money; it's just the individuals or political parties that change. There are always going to be at least two sides to any issue and always people working to ensure that their side wins. As J. D. Williams, my first boss, said, "We work with who the people send us." And that can change every two years.

Like many jobs, lobbying involves long hours and hard work. In many ways, lobbyists are never off duty. Many times, a lobbyist has little notice of when issues will be called to a day's agenda in Congress. That was just the way the Congress worked. A lobbyist must understand all aspects of the issue and its impact on the interested parties and the public and be able to explain it in under three minutes—sometimes while in an elevator or walking with a member of Congress to vote.

As a lobbyist, you develop constituencies that support your position. You meet with members of Congress and their staffs and identify someone who will sponsor legislation to support your issue. You must give them a reason to support your issue, whether that issue is high profile or of little interest to most people.

A major part of lobbying is getting to know the members of Congress and their staff members and the issues they care about. Before the rules changed in 2007, lobbyists used many ways to get to know staff members. A big part of lobbying was access, and in the years when Ron was actively lobbying with members of Congress, our townhouse, one block from the US Senate buildings, was a great location to host fundraisers for election campaigns. During that time, it wasn't unusual for us to host four to six fundraisers a month in our home. While these gatherings were effective, they were also expensive. Contributing to candidates' campaigns was like investing in your business, and politics was our business. And invest we did to the tune of the maximum allowed by law in some election cycles. We only contributed to Democratic candidates we liked, some of whom won and some who lost. Some would become our friends.

One of the perils of lobbying is that you can put a year of effort into a piece of legislation, have most people on board, and find that, during the final hour of a legislative committee, compromises were reached, and your legislation didn't make the cut to the final bill. These are the long hours of boredom punctuated by moments of sheer terror. With a stroke of a pen, your issue is crossed off the list at three o'clock in the morning, while you are waiting in the halls of Congress, sometimes sitting on the marble floors or pacing, waiting for the thumbs-up or down. If you get a thumbs-up, a sleepless night is worth it. Your client is happy, and you have earned your fee. If you get a thumbs-down, you start all over again.

When I first came to Washington in 1977 and began to work for J. D. Williams, I had never heard of lobbying and had no idea what it was or what lobbyists did. As it turned out, there was no better place to learn than in the office where I was working. J. D., along with Tommy Boggs, son of former House Majority Leader Hale Boggs, who died in a plane crash while he was in office, were senior members of the two preeminent legislative/law firms in town.

Working at J. D.'s law firm was my first real job after college. I had never taken a government course in high school or college, so this was all new, daunting, and exciting for me. I attended events with members of Congress most people only saw on television or read about in the news. Access to these people was heady stuff for a young woman in her early twenties. In the first published photo ever taken of me, I was talking with Massachusetts Democrat Tip O'Neill, then Speaker of the House, at an event J. D. was hosting at the Botanic Garden. Although working for J. D. Williams could

97

be difficult, I was a quick study. And working for J. D. and attending all the congressional events did have its perks: I don't think I ever paid for a meal, and food was served at most of these events!

I was working for J. D. just after the Watergate scandal, and campaign rules had changed. Among other changes, effective April 1972, federal campaign law required full reporting of campaign contribution expenditures and limited spending on media advertisements. Beginning in 1974, campaign finance law limited individual contributions to candidates for federal office to $1,000 for each primary, general election, and runoff; political action committees (PACs) were limited to $5,000. And, beginning in 1974, candidates, political parties, and others who spent money in elections were required to file campaign finance reports with the Federal Election Commission. Campaign finance reform was designed to restore public confidence after the Watergate scandals. While these changes seemed major, they became watered down over time, as the public became aware in the aftermath of the Jack Abramoff scandal in 2006, when the term *lobbyist* became a dirty word.

As many would tell me over the years, Ron was one of the best at clearly defining his position and its ramifications to his clients and the members of Congress. The prominent *National Journal* even listed him as one of the top twenty Democratic Senate lobbyists. He could succinctly lay out the position he was advocating, while pointing out its political pros and cons. But most importantly, Ron was unfailingly honest and always acted with integrity.

Ron had lived and breathed politics for almost twenty years before I met him. He had taught political science at the college level and managed election campaigns all over the country. His job at Burger King was a jump from electoral politics to legislative politics. Eventually, I would jump headfirst into that world as well.

While working for Burger King Corporation, Ron was responsible for protecting the company's interest at both the federal and the state levels. He represented the interests of both the corporation and its hundreds of franchisees. It was a big job, and he was always traveling, mostly to Washington. There were numerous issues Burger King cared about, especially those dealing with tax laws and reform. During the 1970s was when Ron first focused on a new (at that time) tax issue, the Targeted Jobs Tax Credit (TJTC), later renamed the Work Opportunity Tax Credit (WOTC). He maintained his interest in this issue for the rest of his career. The tax credit was designed to help individuals from certain targeted groups that faced barriers to employment by awarding a tax credit to companies who hired those individuals. Something that seemed a small issue was worth a lot of money to the bottom line of the corporation and their franchisees. It also helped many harder-to-employ individuals get jobs, particularly during times of higher unemployment, while helping the companies that hired them. It was a win-win for all.

WOTC was first enacted in 1978, while Jimmy Carter was president, and went into effect for tax years beginning 1979. Not only did it save the corporation and its franchisees a lot of money, it also helped employ many disadvantaged folks. First enacted for only two years, WOTC has been extended many times since, although on several occasions it expired for a number of months before being reauthorized. Ron helped to organize and enlist help from many

99

large corporations and those who facilitated filing the tax credits. Since tax credits cost the government money, keeping them can be difficult, especially during times when the federal budget is being cut, as happened during the Reagan administration in 1981–82 and again in 1985–86.

Ron worked with clients on WOTC until he retired in November 2016. He also worked on a variety of tax and healthcare issues for such clients as Campbell Soup Company, Barclays Bank, pharmaceutical companies, and the Los Angeles Raiders and the Washington Redskins football teams. He worked for foreign countries like Malta and international companies, such as Sportingbet, the largest internet gaming company based in the UK. But he never worked harder for an issue than for WOTC, and even though he got tired of working on the same issue for so many years, he continued to do so because he believed in it.

In 2001, while Ron was working at the law firm Greenberg Traurig, he was asked to help other members of the firm recruit the now infamous Jack Abramoff. Abramoff had just been dubbed "Washington's Super Lobbyist" by *Fortune* magazine, and many considered him a big hire for any firm. He would bring with him several very large clients, and he had major ties to Republican leadership in the Congress and the White House. At the time, there was no hint of the scandals that would follow him.

As time went on and Abramoff's team grew, Ron began to get suspicious about where money was going and backed off doing work for Abramoff's clients. Ron's reputation and integrity were an important part of how he defined himself, and he was worried about the dealings of Abramoff and his coworkers and outside consultants. Before Abramoff was asked to resign from Greenberg Traurig in 2004, he had opened two restaurants, bought a fleet of casino boats, produced two Hollywood movies, leased four arena and sta-dium skyboxes, and funded an Orthodox Jewish boys' school in Maryland. He collected tens of millions of dollars from Indian tribes to help pay for those purchases, as well as for lavish golf trips to Scotland and the Pacific Island of Saipan. He hired powerful allies from the Christian Right and archi-tects of the Republican Revolution like Grover Norquist and helped fund the public relations firm founded by Mike Scan-lon, where he directed huge funds for grassroots efforts.

By 2003, the Senate Indian Affairs Committee began hear-ing complaints about Abramoff and the million-dollar fees he was receiving. The Native American tribes who hired him were also funneling large amounts of money to Republicans, when they traditionally donated to Democrats. By the spring of 2004, investigations were launched by the Senate and the Justice Department.

In 2004, Ron and his clients, wanting nothing to do with the developing scandal, left Greenberg for Buchanan Inger-soll LLC, a Pittsburgh-based firm, where he would head their legislative practice. He was happy to be with a new firm and away from the scandal that plagued Abramoff and the firm.

In 2005, in an interview with an NPR reporter, Ron quoted Abramoff as having said, "If you want to make a deal, if you want to compromise, then you ought to hire some-body else, but if you want to win, you ought to hire us." Ron commented, "Given what they were charging, given what they had told the client they were going to do, they abso-lutely could not fail. They had to win every fight. And for the most part they did."

An article in January 2006 in *Washington Monthly* laid it out: "It's now clear that the GOP strategy for limiting dam-age from the Abramoff scandal is to employ the 'Democrats were doing it too' defense." So, Abramoff and his team of Republican operatives were now trying to implicate my husband and other of his colleagues as part of their efforts. They talked about Ron's and my contributions to Senators Reid, Dorgan, Lincoln, and Pryor. Most of this information began with reporter John Solomon, who worked at the Associated Press at the time. Solomon seemed desperate to involve Senate Majority Leader Harry Reid, and he wrote story after story saying that Senator Reid and Ron were doing the same as Abramoff and the Republican members he supported. It didn't matter Ron had volunteered for Reid for three weeks in Nevada in 1994, long before Abramoff entered the scene. It didn't matter the political contributions we gave these senators happened before 2000.

It was a horrible time for Ron. We called a friend who we knew was the best in the field of crisis management and asked for his advice about stopping the lies and half-truths. His advice was to keep quiet and lay low until the scandal passed. The end of this story came when Abramoff was tried, found guilty of three felony charges, conspiracy, corruption, mail fraud, and tax evasion, and sentenced to forty-eight months in prison.

Just as happened after the Watergate scandal thirty years before, what followed was a comprehensive lobbying and ethics reform, the Honest Leadership and Open Government Act, which was passed by the Senate in August 2007. It was called the single most sweeping congressional reform since Watergate. One of those reforms would require lobbyists to disclose all their campaign contributions twice a year and file lobbying reports to Congress quarterly that would be available to the public.

Meanwhile Ron was being noticed by more national law firms, where he was hired to run the government affairs practice. This work led to more international clients and notoriety. He was representing Fortune 100 companies in the United States and international companies and countries.

One of the partners in the firm's New York office handled real estate work for Donald Trump and the Trump Organization, and they asked Ron to go to New York to discuss a project for Trump. Trump wanted to build a casino with a Native American Tribe, but the tribe had to receive federal recognition. Ron and his partners went to work with the Congress and Bureau of Indian Affairs. They were successful and finished the project, but in usual Trump fashion, as Ron and the rest of the world would later discover, the firm had yet to receive payment for Ron's services to the tune of over $600,000. Ron was asked to travel New York and meet directly with Trump to go over the project and request payment. When they met, Ron laid out the work that was done with Trump, then asked for payment.

Donald Trump's response was something that would become quite expected: "It should be so prestigious in Washington to represent me, you shouldn't require payment." Ron's response was, "BULLSHIT!"

Incensed that someone would speak to him that way, Trump stood and blustered out of the room. Ron sat and waited for a very long time. He was determined not to leave Trump's office without full payment. The partner who had come to the meeting with Ron left the room to talk to Trump. We never knew what he said, but apparently it was enough: he came back half an hour later with a check for the full amount. Ron made a beeline to his

New York office with instructions to deposit the check immediately!

Ron was so proud of that moment, he relayed that story time and time again until it appeared later in *The Washington Post* and in a book about Trump.

# 13

## A Tap on My Shoulder and a Defining Life Year

Waking up one Saturday morning in August 2015, with my Ron lying next to me in bed and our dogs circling to go outside and have breakfast, I was content, happy, and loved. I knew who I was, and I had more than I could ever wish for. I had a loving husband who could be a tough guy in business but was a teddy bear with me. We had successful careers; we were healthy and happy, with purpose in our lives.

Ron and I had been married for thirty-six years. We were each other's best friend, lover, and supporter. We had formed a modern, blended family with his three children, our grandchildren, my father and stepmother, and my two half-siblings and nieces and nephews. While our family members lived in different states, we made it a point to try and see each other often; many of those times we gathered around Ron's and my dining room table enjoying a home-cooked feast.

We had just returned from our summer adventure, this year to Ecuador. We visited the equator, took a train through the indigenous areas of Ecuador, and spent a few fascinating days touring the Galapagos Islands and marveling at the animals inhabiting them. I had the idea of the train trip through Ecuador, as Ron loved train travel, and the Galapagos addition was Ron's idea, as he knew of my desire to go there to see the wide diversity of animal species. Most of our away vacations took place in August, when Congress is on summer break; it is also Ron's birthday month. Our sixteen-year-old, hundred-pound labradoodle, Corey, managed to stay alive while we were away, but it became clear, shortly after our return, that his time had come. It broke our hearts, particularly Ron's, as Corey was his dog. We called our kindly British vet to the house so we could be with Corey when he simply fell asleep. Ron couldn't handle it, so he said goodbye to Corey with a hug and went to our bedroom to grieve. We didn't talk about it—talking about these things was not Ron's habit. After all, as we would say, Corey had survived long past his expiration date.

On this Saturday morning, having fed the other dogs and let them outside, I made breakfast as usual—blueberry waffles, Ron's favorite. Ron was still in the family room reading the paper and watching sports news on the television, so I went back to shower before it was time for errands and chores. I had no inkling of what would happen next or what it might portend for the future.

We had a wonderfully designed master bath that had a glassed-in shower surrounded by a large, curved stone entryway with tumbled marble on the walls and floor. I loved that shower. Every time I was in it, I felt like I was in old

Europe somewhere. As I was washing my hair, I felt a hand on my shoulder. I wasn't startled; I simply turned, expecting to see Ron standing there in the shower with me. When I saw I was alone, I wasn't fearful; I had felt something kind in that touch, something real and comforting. I believe it was my mother's spirit sending me a message, but I didn't have a clue as to what it might mean.

The call came later that morning. Karen's boyfriend, Morris, called to tell us Karen had collapsed, unable to breathe, and had been rushed by ambulance to the hospital. Over the years, Karen would travel many times by ambulance to the hospital. Her alcoholism was out of control, she was divorced, and rarely did her children want to visit her. Ron had paid for alcohol addiction clinics and therapy many times over the years, but none of the treatments were successful.

Ron flew to Miami, where Karen was living, on the first flight he could get. The doctors told him her body was finally shutting down after many years of living with the effects of cirrhosis of the liver. Ron and Karen's daughter, Kristin, decided to take her off the ventilator, and they waited throughout the night, holding her hands and telling her she was loved, until she passed. I flew to Miami the next day, and we gathered with Karen's children, her ex-husband, and her mother-in-law and talked about the better times we all had. Ron never cried or showed much emotion, but the grief showed in his face.

Not two months later, in late October, I would lose my father from dementia. For almost sixty years, he had been a constant in my life, and for a while in my childhood, he was the only parent I had. After he and my stepmother moved to an assisted-living facility, I had driven to Pittsburgh to bring them to visit with Ron and me and their two dogs, who were now living with Ron and me. Dad had just come from the doctor because he wasn't feeling well or eating anything, but my stepmother said there was nothing serious.

Over the next couple of days, his condition worsened to the point that he was unable to move. I decided something was very wrong and called an ambulance to help me get him into my car to drive him back to the hospital in Pittsburgh, where his doctors and medical records were. On the ride home, Dad looked out the front window and pointed to the sky. Barb said, "Tony, are you pointing to heaven and seeing Julie?" (Julie was my deceased mother.)

After a couple days in the hospital, Dad would say his last words, "All my family is here." All his children and grandchildren were there. Ron was in Washington, and luckily my childhood friend Heidi was there for support. My nephew Gage played his guitar and sang a song for Dad, then we all talked to him, said our goodbyes individually, and told him how much he was loved and gave him the biggest hugs to send him on his journey.

Ron and I made our way quietly and somberly to Pittsburgh for the funeral home gatherings and service. I had so much I wanted to say about the man who had gently guided and loved me, but I wasn't sure I could adequately express how much he meant to me without breaking down emotionally. To prepare myself, I reflected on a long-ago event to gain courage.

The event was my confirmation, where my father provided an example of courage that helped me get through what I wanted to say at the funeral. He had a stutter and never chose to speak before an audience, but to my surprise, he appeared at the lectern on this Sunday. He wanted to surprise me by speaking in front of the entire congregation without stuttering. Later, I learned he practiced for hours on the words he spoke that day. He did it without a stutter and thus set a tremendous example for me. I worked for hours and hours to get his eulogy just right, and I delivered it without a stumble. He would be as proud of me as I had been of him.

Those three months in 2015—August through October—would be the most challenging either of us had endured up to then.

# 14

## Leading by Example

For almost ten years, I talked to women about running for public office, but it was never something I considered for myself. I was most comfortable working behind the scenes, letting others do the speaking. I was good at plotting, planning, and executing. I was never the mouthpiece. What did I have to say? Would anyone listen? Was I brave enough to speak about what I cared about and my life experiences? And who the hell would care?

In late December 2016, the electoral college winner for president was Donald Trump. Hillary Clinton had won the popular vote but would not become our first woman president. Ron and I watched the election returns with disbelief. His earlier experience with Donald Trump led him to have a palpable disdain for the man. I had asked pollster after pollster for reassurance Hillary would win, and they had given it to me. Surely, Donald Trump couldn't win, but he did.

I was in good company, as many other women, and many men, were appalled. We would now have an admitted "pussy grabber" in the White House, and he was proud of it! How could any woman with any self-respect have voted for that man? After a brief time hiding under the covers, drinking wine, and listening to the news reports with a strong desire to smash the television screen, I picked myself up and began working at taking back our country. Women from all walks of life seemed ready to fight for their rights: stay-at-home moms, young women, women in their seventies and eighties, women who never considered themselves activists. And we took to the streets to protest the results. Something powerful had begun because of Trump's win and would continue for years to come.

Ron was glad he had retired in November; he wanted nothing to do with the government under a Trump administration. He knew how underhanded and narcissistic Trump could be. We talked about Ron trying to get some clients, but instead of looking for clients, he would sit for hours in front of the computer and just read the news. I worried what we would do to make a living, since his income had been more than triple what I was earning, but now Republicans controlled the White House, as well as the Senate and the House—a trifecta. Work for Democrats was going to be in short supply. Ron had worked hard for many years so we could have the life we wanted. Now, it was my turn to make sure, if I could, that we would remain financially stable and secure. It was a scary time for me as a wife, caregiver, breadwinner, and lover.

Virginia, unlike every state in the country except for New Jersey, has elections every year, and in 2017, we were going to have a big one. It was an election year for the entire House of Delegates and our statewide offices: governor, lieutenant governor, and attorney general. While many women stood up to run for the House of Delegates seats, not one woman came forward to run for statewide office.

Since the Virginia governor is limited to one four-year term, the current Democratic lieutenant governor was going to run for governor, and the current Democratic attorney general was going to run for reelection. The only possible statewide opportunity was for the office of lieutenant governor.

Out of nowhere it seemed, it occurred to me that maybe I could run. I said it quietly and hesitantly in my head. For years, I had been telling women to be brave, take a chance, and run; now maybe it was time to take my own advice and lead by example. I couldn't say it out loud yet, but I let it bounce around in my head for a while. When I called downstairs to Ron and said, "What about if I run for lieutenant governor?" His response was immediate: "Go for it!"

What was I thinking? I hated talking about myself. I hated public speaking. How were we going to make a living during the campaign? All very good questions; add to that, the lieutenant governor's salary was $17,500 a year. If I won, we couldn't live on that salary. These questions and others ran through my mind constantly, and then I would ask myself, "What the hell am I thinking?" But then I thought that maybe Ron would get engaged in the campaign and work through his depression to find purpose again. That was my hope at least.

Christmas was just a few days away when I started to make a few calls to tell some friends what I was thinking. Since the Democratic primary was in early June, I had to start organizing if I was going to run. The first reactions I got were shocked, as I had never expressed a desire to run for office. Sure, I was experienced, but I was a "pol," not an expert on state issues. Of course, I knew what the issues were, but no one had ever heard me address them. As time passed, political allies agreed I knew Virginia and had the political background I needed and could probably raise the money I would need, so supporters began signing up. On December 20, I followed up by sending an email to every Democrat in Virginia whose email I could get. I told them I was considering a run and why. I was experienced, I knew the state and people politically, and I asked for their thoughts on how we could accomplish more, with better solutions, for all Virginians.

By January 6, 2017, my potential candidacy made headlines in *The Washington Post*: "Former Biden chief of staff files to run for Virginia lieutenant governor." Well, I thought, there was no turning back now, so it was time for Ron and me to fasten our seat belts for the ride ahead. In addition to *The Washington Post*, the story of my upcoming bid for office appeared in papers throughout Virginia and across the country because Biden had been vice president for eight years.

Meanwhile, I was quietly in panic mode, but Ron just kept saying, "You can do it," "I'll help you," "I'm behind you"—and he was. He gave me immeasurable courage and confidence. My largest and longest-term client read the headlines and called me to ask if the news story was true. I told him I had not made a firm decision yet, but if they would support this effort and let me continue to work and get paid by them, I would be able to move forward. They were wholeheartedly behind me.

January was a big month. I had to form a campaign committee, raise money, hire staff, plan my announcement, and outline a media strategy. Every waking hour was filled with political and fundraising calls, strategy meetings, schedule planning, and structuring my campaign. I needed to hire people who would understand what I stood for and my work ethic. On January 14, 2017, I delivered my first speech as a candidate to the Virginia Democratic Party Women's Caucus. I had worked and reworked that speech repeatedly.

I needed to find my voice to deliver the speech pitch perfect. It had to be smart; it had to be serious and thoughtful; it had to be personal and heartfelt; and it had to have funny lines. I had to talk about myself. I wasn't guiding other candidates; it was me now, and my head was spinning.

As a woman candidate I had to pay attention to my personal appearance. Part of the double standard for women is that we can't wear anything too fashionable or too flashy or too girly; hair and makeup must be simple and just so. I preached these things to the women we trained at EmergeVA, and now I was the one who had to follow my own advice!

This speech would be my introduction, outlining who I was, why I was running, and why I deserved support; it would also be the first time I would appear with the other candidates for governor and lieutenant governor and hear their pitches. There were two other Democratic candidates for lieutenant governor: Gene Rossi, a newcomer in Virginia political circles who had been a US attorney, and Justin Fairfax, who had been a candidate for attorney general in Virginia four years earlier and had almost beaten the current AG. He was an African American lawyer who had worked in the US Attorney's office under Gene Rossi. Unfortunately for Gene, there just wasn't a lane for his candidacy. But Justin was another matter; he had run statewide before, so he was widely known in Democratic circles, and as an African American, he would win a lot of minority votes in the Democratic primary. Numerous political folks told me there was no way I would beat Justin, but I couldn't let that deter me. I didn't really consider what the results in the primary would mean; it was just something I had to do. This was a somewhat impractical and shocking statement coming from someone who had worked for many years on election campaigns and knew the only thing that mattered was who won.

I began my speech with a quote from Reba McEntire: "In order to succeed in life you need three things: a wishbone, a backbone, and a funny bone."[2] I continued by saying that nine years earlier at this same gathering, Mary Sue Terry and I had decided we needed to do something to help women become elected leaders, so we formed The Farm Team that later became EmergeVA. I talked about my background, my work, my family, and my core beliefs. I talked about losing my stepdaughter to addiction and the need for access to better treatment and mental health services.

I had to come up with something great as a closer to the speech—something memorable. I researched the history of lieutenant governors in Virginia. The closing sentence to my speech was, "Virginia has had forty lieutenant governors: six Johns, four Jameses, two Roberts, one L. Douglas, and no Marys, Louises, or Susans." This became what people remembered from that speech, and women loved it. I would conclude with that sentence at every campaign stop I made to the point where people would wait for the end of my speech and say it with me.

The campaign had begun. I hired the renowned producer Martha McKenna, who produced the introductory video announcing my candidacy that focused on the women's march, our love of family and dedication to helping families with mental health care, and greater economic opportunities. For the next four months, I went everywhere and anywhere across Virginia to speak with small groups, large groups, labor groups, women's groups, and business groups. I participated in debates and forums. At this point, I was leading every public poll, as many women would respond when questioned about the candidate they favored: "the woman!" They may not have remembered my name, but they knew I was the only woman in the race. I was surprised with the results, but having been involved in politics for as long as I had been, I knew these polls really didn't mean anything and I didn't have the money to do my own poll, so we just flew by the seat of our pants. At the back of my mind, I was aware how many African Americans voted in the Democratic primary, and I had only been in the race for a few months with only a fraction of the money Justin Fairfax had, but we persevered.

I was growing more comfortable talking about myself, who I was, and why I thought I was the best person to lead the Commonwealth. I heard that my hair was frizzy; I didn't smile enough. But most importantly, I heard from people who had lost family members to addiction. They would thank me quietly for talking about Karen's death from addiction, often with a hug and sometimes with tears in their eyes. This was the most gratifying thing that happened to me during the entire campaign. They, and I, didn't feel so alone. Ron almost never came with me to these events, as someone had to stay home and take care of the dogs. I did wonder if those encounters would have given him some comfort as well.

With less than one month to go in the primary, one of my campaign staffers came to me with something that would be very bold and provocative in a state that had once been the capital of the Confederacy: calling for removing the statues of the military generals who had led the war for the South and for slavery, that were so prominent in Richmond and around the state. I told them this was something I had to consider overnight and talk to Ron about. Ron told me that Sarge Reynolds, the lieutenant governor for whom he had worked in the 1970s, would drive past those statues on Monument Avenue in Richmond every day. Reynolds talked about their meaning—they were meant to oppress—and how they affected people of color. Ron agreed it would be provocative and risky to take this position, but it needed to be said and done. I believed he was correct, and I agreed.

I had hired Adam Parkhomenko to oversee my campaign. While he had never managed a campaign, he was well-known for having organized the "Ready for Hillary" PAC previously, and I knew he could help spread my candidacy not only across Virginia, but nationally. He brought with him a couple other staffers, of whom Seth Bringman from the Ohio Democratic Party handled press relations. I had already hired Andrew Cyphers, fundraiser extraordinaire, August Christian as field director, and Herb Smith as deputy manager. The next morning, I told Adam and Seth I was going to do it, and we began to work on my statement. It said, "If I am elected lieutenant governor, I will ask the governor to appoint me to lead a commission charged with taking down Confederate monuments as well as renaming Confederate-themed highways and public buildings ... our taxpayer dollars should not be used to celebrate a rebellion against the United States of America, a rebellion intended to maintain slavery."

Up to this point, no candidate had discussed removal of these statues, and my position statement created a shock wave that was heard around the state and beyond. It became all anyone was talking about, and not always in a positive manner. In many ways, I was caught off guard by the intensity of the discussion, although in hindsight I shouldn't have been. There were strong opposing views on these monuments. Many believed the monuments were symbols of slavery and racial oppression, while many others saw them as a tribute to Southern heritage. Days after my press statement and news coverage, the *Richmond Times-Dispatch* posted a poll asking its readers whether the monuments should be removed. The results were 40 percent in favor of removal and 58 percent against. It was interesting to watch how many of our leading statewide elected Democrats kept their mouths shut or even openly disagreed.

Shortly after this, I received a strange call on our home phone. The man asked if I was Susan Platt and then repeated our home address. It was a warning of sorts, as he said our address was posted online, and he wanted to see if it was correct. I got on the computer, and with the help of several campaign aides, found the horrifying post.

There was the photo of me that we used on my campaign website with a noose alongside it. The post continued, listing my home phone and address, then said my house should be looted and burned down. My neighbor across the street, who had been a Secret Service agent, came over to tell me she had seen two cars taking turns on watch at the end of our property. Now it was getting serious. I called the Virginia attorney general, who said he would contact the FBI, and my local supervisor to contact the police captain for my area of Fairfax County. The captain told me they were aware of this group on the dark web but couldn't verify their names. I was calm and not particularly afraid, but I was sure mad. Ron was acting as guard, sitting on the couch with his shotgun in hand, at the ready. That was almost scarier than the online threat! The police set up a routine of patrolling our home and property. After a few days, the strange cars disappeared and everything calmed down. The Democratic primary was two weeks away.

The day of the primary, Ron and I went to vote together. During the day I traveled to the various polling locations throughout Fairfax County, and Ron went to a polling place inside a senior living facility handing out my literature and asking them to vote for his wife. I heard about this, and everyone said he was so proud of me and what we accomplished.

Before this day, I hadn't considered how I would feel about the outcome. As I have said many times before, I was just running. When the results began to come in, it became apparent we would come up short. I begrudgingly called Justin Fairfax, the winner, and congratulated him. I say begrudgingly because of his campaign of disinformation. I didn't operate that way and found it the reason so many people hated politics. But I guess he felt he needed to do it to stop me, and it worked. The results were counted, and Justin Fairfax won with 252,291 votes, or 49.22 percent; Susan Platt had 200,537 votes, or 39.12 percent; and Gene Rossi got 59,797 votes, 11.66 percent.

I was proud of the four-month underfunded campaign we ran and felt I could hold my head up high. In the end, I am so glad I had the experience, for myself and for women who might decide to run for office in the future. I had done something I never thought I would have the courage to do. While I didn't win my campaign, many women did win delegate races across Virginia, and most of them were our fellow EmergeVA grads. We were all bold and threw caution to the wind, turning anger into positive change.

# 15

---

# Roar

For most of my life, I felt I didn't have much to say that others would care about. In my work on the election campaigns of others, I was able to talk about their views. But in my campaign for lieutenant governor, I was suddenly speaking about myself and my candidacy, and I realized there were issues I could speak about that were important to women.

Shortly after my political campaign, I was a guest several times on a conservative political radio show to talk about my campaign, and I personally liked the host, leaving aside his politics. He had gone all in for Trump for president, but he had a pretty good feel for what was happening politically in Virginia, and he was fair to me. After learning through a press release that Gene Rossi, the opponent in my primary race who got the least votes, would be hosting a show on this station, I asked myself why he was offered a show instead of me. I called the host who had interviewed me, who was also the owner of the radio station, and asked him why he didn't have any women on his network. He responded that he thought I wouldn't be interested in hosting a show, so he hadn't asked. I'm not sure that was the whole story, but when he asked if I would do it, I said, "Hell, yes!"

My show would air for sixty minutes at 9 a.m. on Saturday mornings. At first, I thought this was a horrible time. But after some research, I found it was a great time for women. Even if they had full-time jobs, they would usually be at home on Saturday morning. If they had children, they would be in the car driving them to their weekend activities. So, with a lot of trepidation about my ability to pull this off, but also excitement at a new challenge, I aired my first show, "PLATT-i-TUDES, Find Your Roar," for and about women.

The radio station was outside Norfolk, a three-hour drive from northern Virginia; I had to leave my house before 6 a.m. to get there, do the show for an hour, then drive home. It was a long day.

This show was a first for a woman in Virginia, and I was a high-profile person, so I worked hard to find the right words and tone for the show. In the first episode of the show, I talked about finding my voice when I ran for political office. I encouraged women to speak up and say that they wanted respect for their achievements and to be rewarded fairly for their work We needed to speak our desires clearly and loudly—we needed to roar.

My father had always told me he was determined that I would not be defined by my sex but by my hard work and determination, and my husband echoed that. As I got older, I found out what a leader my mother had been: she was valedictorian of her graduating class and became the first woman auditor in the Navy. I wanted to make her proud. I had helped women interested in pursuing politics to find their voice, and I wanted more women to become engaged and speak out as their rights were being threatened.

The topics on the show were as varied as the guests I interviewed. I began my show not only with several women leaders in the state senate and state house, but also a man, Congressman Bobby Scott, who had been Virginia's only African American member of Congress. I was all about women, but we needed our male leaders to walk to ensure we would continue our progress.

Unlike syndicated radio shows, there were no producers, writers, or talent bookers for my show. I wore all the hats: deciding on the topic, finding and confirming the speakers, researching the topic, and determining the questions to ask every week. And I still had to make a living at my day job.

Several shows stand out in my mind. In Richmond, I interviewed Lori Haas, whose daughter was shot and wounded at the massacre on Virginia Tech's campus in April 2007, where thirty-three people lost their lives. Lori's daughter survived, but as part of her emotional healing and to help prevent further shootings, Lori volunteered for advocacy groups, dedicating herself to preventing more gun violence. She went on to become state director of the Virginia Coalition to Stop Gun Violence.

I drove seven hours to Bristol, Tennessee, just over the far southwest border with Virginia, to interview a woman who had been living in a tent, sleeping on a cot in the cold for over one hundred days at that point. She was a military veteran and a grandmother, protesting a large regional hospital system that was closing several smaller regional emergency care facilities in rural Virginia as cost-saving measures. As a result of these closures, there was nowhere to go within a sixty-mile radius for those in medical crisis. As the EMTs told me, the sixty minutes it took to get to a larger hospital was the golden hour in which to save patients. This woman continued her protest for 365 days, and what started out as one determined woman became a volunteer corps of local folks who would take turns keeping vigil with her day and night. There were stories written about her in *The New York Times* and many other newspapers and periodicals. As a result, the hospital was forced to reconsider some of the closures and add in smaller facilities that could at least stabilize someone for transport.

I heard about a free market in the little town of Independence, Virginia, population one thousand people. The free market was a project begun by a woman who had retired from a government job in DC and had moved back to her hometown. The idea of the market was to serve the community by collecting unwanted items to give to those who needed them. She formed a nonprofit and found volunteers to help. She found an old auto service station that the owner allowed her to use rent free. She spread the word, and the donations came pouring in. They accepted gently used items ranging from kitchen tools and appliances, furniture, and bedding, to a medical lending library for rehab equipment and more. And everything was always free. She was and is able to help so many families with many necessities they would never have been able to afford.

Sadly, while I loved doing the show and met some amazing women, the amount of work involved with a weekly radio show, when the only pay I received was from advertisements, was too much to handle in addition to the client work I was doing to keep afloat, so I stopped.

As a result of my career in politics and my radio program, I was asked to speak on the steps of the Lincoln Memorial at the second Women's March on Washington in January 2018. The crowd would not be the almost one million marchers who attended the first march in January 2017, but there would be a large number and a lot of media coverage.

I wasn't afraid to speak, but I wanted my speech to be relevant and have an impact. When I arrived at the monument, I looked up at Lincoln and down at the lawn surrounding the reflecting pool to the crowd that was developing. In spite of the crowd, I was cool as a cucumber. I began delivering my speech, and the crowd responded enthusiastically, clapping and whooping and hollering. It was quite a heady experience. I wished my dad were still alive to see me give that speech.

The speech was broadcast live on networks and C-SPAN, and shortly after giving it, I got an email from a producer in New York who said his client, jazz singer Karrin Allyson, was recording an album celebrating the centennial of women's suffrage and wanted to include part of my speech at the beginning of one of her songs, "The March of the Women." How cool was that! I signed off any rights to it immediately and couldn't wait to hear it and play it for my grandchildren.

# 16

---

# The Last Years

Most of the memories of my time with Ron are of the full life we had together; I remember how we nurtured, pushed, and cherished each other; how we laughed and bickered; how we explored the world and each other; and how we dealt with grief and depression. But our last few years together were filled with challenges.

Ron and I had both experienced grief and loss. Ron's grandmother died not long before we were married. Mama Barker was a warm and loving presence in his life, an important counterbalance to his cold and remote mother. But she wasn't the first: when he was younger, his favorite uncle was killed by a train on Christmas Eve. Later, as a young husband, Ron discovered Martin, his third child, dead in his crib, a tiny victim of sudden infant death syndrome. This was a loss he never really got over, but, along with the other losses in his life, he rarely talked about it. This ultimately would also prove to make things more difficult toward the end of his life.

Ron's folks lived in our weekend house on High Knob for several years until his mother died in 1992 of reoccurrence of breast cancer. We sold the house on High Knob and moved Ron's dad to live with us in Great Falls. It was a wonderful bonding time for the two men. I was so glad to see their relationship deepen during that time. Their relationship never had the closeness they had recently developed.

Years earlier, Hook made daily visits to his stepmother, who was living in a nursing home, combing her hair and showing her in other small ways that she was loved. But Ron promised his dad he would never place him in a nursing home. The first thing Ron said after his death was, "I promised him he would never live in a nursing home. And I made good on that promise."

For both Ron and me, 2015 was the worst year emotionally of our lives together: Ron's daughter died from the effects of alcohol in August of that year, and my father died of dementia in October. Losing my dad was a terrible blow. He had been my protection for my entire life. Growing up, he was my world.

For Ron, Karen's death proved to be something from which he would never recover. The first year after Karen's death, Ron's interest in work declined dramatically. He was still staying in his apartment in DC from Monday through Thursday, but there were times I would call him at 10 or 11 a.m. and he would not yet have left for the office. For a man who had risen early every morning ready to charge through the day, this was a dramatic change. The next year, when the firm he was with was going to cut his salary, he decided to retire. As he said at the time, it was a stupid thing to do; his ego made him do it.

For the first few months of his retirement, he read novels, watched movies, and was generally detached. His motivation was missing. Around this time I discovered he had spent almost everything we had in retirement savings trying to save Karen. Some might question how I could not know this, but I relied on him to handle our finances. He didn't spend the money on frivolous things; he was paying for treatments for Karen in alcohol rehabilitation facilities and for her living expenses, medical expenses, and more. I was aware he was helping Karen financially, but I had no idea how much money he was spending.

After her death, most days Ron sat on the couch, barely moving. Nothing interested him. His behavior was frustrating and maddening and incomprehensible for me. I couldn't understand why he cared so little or was so cavalier about our financial situation. I was still consulting, as I had been doing for the last few years, but that income wasn't nearly enough to maintain our home and everything else. It was a very frightening time for me. My husband, my partner, could no longer be counted on for emotional or financial support. He was stuck. He said he wanted to do things, but he just couldn't seem to move. He finally said something that stunned me, "I've lost my purpose." I had no idea what that could mean. As I saw it, we were our purpose; our family was our purpose; our work was our purpose. But I eventually came to understand that Ron felt he was responsible for the lives of his children. He believed he was supposed to help them and see them through the bad times, and with Karen, in his own eyes, he had failed. He believed he was responsible for her disease and her death, and nothing could convince him otherwise. He didn't believe in himself anymore. Things had to change.

To save money, we sold the house in Great Falls and bought a smaller home in Leesburg. Ron enrolled in a two-week outpatient program for depression. He started seeing a psychiatrist weekly. The doctor changed his prescription over and over, yet nothing changed. I tried to get him to write, to call friends, to work, to exercise—anything to get him interested in living again. Eventually, he sat so long that moving or walking became hard. We got a trainer, who was able to get him to walk again, and he seemed to be feeling a little lighter.

Several weeks later, his son, Keith, called with the word that Jeanne, Keith's mother, was in heart failure and was on a ventilator. Within a few short hours of getting the news, Ron stood up and immediately lost his balance. His foot was so swollen he couldn't put weight on it. Something similar had happened to Ron during stressful times but not in many years. When he was changing careers to become a corporate executive, he had symptoms of low-grade fever, transitory swelling joints, and general achiness. He even experienced these symptoms after our marriage. He went through all the tests, and they revealed nothing physically wrong with him that would cause these symptoms. I had been concerned and wanted to figure out something that would help him, but a doctor said it could be stress, that even good things were stressful. He suggested aspirin several times a day for the swelling and pain and Valium once a day for a couple weeks to see if that helped. The treatment worked. We had a diagnosis for the symptoms: emotional stress. That was then.

This time, the stress reaction only got worse. Within a few days, his leg was stiff, and he couldn't move it to walk. I took him to our primary care doctor, and she ordered a physical therapist to come to our home. After working with the therapist for a few weeks, he was able to walk with the help of a walker. But that was ultimately the best he would ever be. A bad urinary tract infection resulting in a hospital stay put him way back. Doctors did a CT scan and found nothing neurological that would cause Ron's inability to walk. Even the nephrologist told Ron he needed to have a better attitude because he saw no physical reason for his symptoms.

Things continued a downhill slide, even after a stint in a physical rehabilitation facility. I told Ron we needed to do something drastic, and he agreed, so he checked into the psychological unit of the hospital. I was an emotional wreck while he was there. I couldn't visit him, and he kept calling me to come get him. He thought he was in Texas and couldn't figure out why he was there. He was heavily drugged and sounded drunk and out of his mind when he called me. But I kept telling him they were going to help him and to give it some time. Those weeks in the hospital did nothing positive for him; when he was discharged, the doctor told me he was still very depressed. I took him to our primary care doctor, and she immediately took him off all the drugs he was taking and put him back on the drugs she had given him before the episode occurred. At this point, Ron was not able to walk at all, nor could he take care of himself.

I felt isolated and helpless and more desperate by the day. I called my childhood friend daily. We had lived next door to each other growing up, and we had been inseparable. We eventually drifted apart as we entered high school and rarely got together during our college years.

My friend called me when she got married—at about the time Ron and I were to marry. When Ron and I moved back to DC, she called to say her younger sister was moving to DC and needed a temporary place to stay while she looked for an apartment. At another time, when I learned from my father that her father had died, I called her immediately to express my sadness. This kind of occasional but regular contact continued for years. Eventually, when her children got older and I was not working on campaigns, we stayed in contact more often. At some point, I suggested we take a trip together, and this became a regular event. In short, we had a friendship that began in childhood and extended until the final days of Ron's illness, when things changed.

During Ron's stay in the psychiatric hospital and after his return home when it was becoming clear he needed more constant care than I could give him, I called her almost daily to be a sounding board. When Ron became even more depressed and withdrawn and we determined it would be good for him to admit himself to the psychiatric ward of the hospital, she and her husband came to be with us as we admitted him.

After Ron was released from his stay in the psychiatric ward and was clearly no better, I felt I had some difficult decisions ahead of me, and I felt more lonely and scared than I could ever remember feeling. But this time when I called her, she said she couldn't listen. I told her maybe it was time we took a break in our friendship, and she agreed. While I have communicated by email and text with her, I haven't talked to her since.

As long as I had known Ron, he was fearless, but now he told me he was afraid of dying. I told him he wasn't dying. He had a urinary tract infection, and he was suffering from depression, but he wasn't dying. I even had his doctors and our psychologist tell him that. But something told him he was.

Ron's condition continued to worsen over the next six months. We had a new psychiatrist, who tried many drugs. This psychiatrist even ordered a gene profile test, which was supposed to tell us which drugs would work the best.

We tried hypnosis for a while too. Nothing worked for the depression, and he continued to get one urinary tract infection after another, which affected his brain chemistry as well. We even tried ketamine infusions; he seemed to get better at first, but then he got worse. Our hope was fading that he would recover. He kept telling me he wanted to recover and believed that he would; he just didn't know how or when. Eventually, he didn't move, he didn't talk; I had to wash him, lift him, feed him.

During the last week of Ron's life, I sat in front of my laptop and started typing. We were supposed to be on vacation at the beach in South Carolina with my brother and his family. Instead, Ron was rushed to the hospital, where days later they told me he would not recover. The waiting for anything good to happen was over, and a kind of despair took its place. But there was something in detailing his life and our life together that became the most important thing I could do at that moment. I didn't have the ability to verbalize what I was feeling, so I wrote it down.

# PART THREE

# THE LOSS

# 17
---
# Alone

In many ways, I have always felt like a fraud. I flew by the seat of my pants and my gut instincts. Mostly, I just kept moving. I looked up to Ron: he had the smarts, the education, the training and experience, and he shared those with me—it was nothing I did. Ron kept telling me I could do anything; he told me I was smart and intuitive and could succeed at anything I put my mind to. Oh, I could point to successes in my life, but those were just a fluke, right? I just got lucky, and, as the saying goes, "timing is everything." I didn't do anything halfway, but I felt as if my successes came because of Ron's support.

Except for the six months following my separation from my first husband, I had never lived alone. Now, in my late sixties, I found myself alone and wondering who I was, what I was doing, what the future looked like, whether I could live alone. And whether I had it in me to start again.

I thought I knew about grieving. I had lost my mother, my father, and my stepmother, who became a wonderful mother and role model for me. Losing your parents is terribly hard, but it's also expected; it's the way life is supposed to go. But losing my life partner was indescribable and shattering. Even though Ron was thirteen years older than me, I always believed I would be the one to go first, since my mother had died at such a young age, while Ron's father and uncles lived well into their late eighties and early nineties.

Some days I woke up shaking, thinking about having to face the day without him. I had to force myself to sit up, move my legs off the bed, and put one foot in front of the other. Some days the only thing that got me up was taking care of my dogs. Thank God for them. Some days I just didn't move. Sometimes I wondered why I needed to keep moving. And sometimes, I felt like punching the next person who told me how strong I was. I love to cook, but I wondered how I could cook only for myself. Things I had loved doing with Ron stopped being enjoyable.

I still sleep on my side of the bed. Luckily, one of my dogs curls up next to me in the empty space, and sometimes he even snores. I still have Ron's toothbrush next to mine in the bathroom, and I keep his comb next to my brush. While I have given away most of his clothing, there are still a few shirts and sweaters and his tuxedo in the closet. I find it comforting to see them when I go to my closet.

When asked if I could describe the best day of our life together, I have no answer because I had almost forty-three years of best days. Filling in the last few days of Ron's life helped me remember the wonderful times of our life together. I never wanted to forget the good times. I hoped that I could take all I had learned and all the wonderful life experiences and use them to feel grateful for what we had together.

When I told my psychologist that I had no idea why I was still here, he said, "There clearly must be more for you to do." I hope I can figure out what that is.

# 18

---

# So This Is Grief

A friend posted on social media, "The feeling of losing your husband simply cannot be understood until you experience it yourself." Nothing truer could be said about this loss.

I do not know how to grieve. I don't know that anyone ever does. For sixty years, since my mother's death, I had run from grief, but it finally caught up with me when my husband died. It sometimes feels as though grief is a verb, because it's forever changing, evolving. It can come in waves when you least expect it, and the speed and movement of those waves can be dizzying. One year of mourning may be what custom tells us appropriate, but I found that grief doesn't have a prescribed timeline. It may change in outward appearance, or it may never end. I continued to go through the motions of living but wondered if at any moment I would tumble into the abyss and never crawl out.

I watched how grief gripped my husband when his daughter, Karen, died from the effects of long-term alcohol abuse.

After his death, I discovered something he had written: "My life ended when my daughter died, and I couldn't save her." In the year following Karen's death, I noticed Ron's lack of energy, focus, and motivation, but he couldn't or wouldn't admit how much her death affected him. Eventually, he told me that he had lost his sense of purpose. He quit moving and finally, after three years, he could not move. He was consumed with what he believed were his failures, and he lost the belief in his own power. And following his death from a broken heart, I have lost mine.

In the first days and weeks following Ron's death, I operated in a fuzzy state of shock. If I let myself, I too could stop moving from grief, just as my husband had, but I had plans to make and tasks to perform related to Ron's death that no one else could shoulder for me. My friends and family gathered around me, but there was nothing they could do. I was with people I loved and who loved me, but I felt more alone than ever before.

I got through the first few days because I did not have a choice. I performed the obligatory tasks of making decisions about a funeral or not, burial service or not, religious service or celebration of life or not. I cried while trying to focus enough to compose an obituary and pick a photo for the newspaper that would be worthy of my husband. I got death certificates that I refused to read. I did not need a reality check; I was living it. And so, the process began, and I kept moving. Some people called but had no idea what to say. I didn't know what to say either. Others didn't call at all, choosing to avoid coming up with something to say or do. I felt like a zombie going through the motions. This is how my father must have felt when my mother died: he still had me but was incomplete without her.

Eventually, the family left and the friends went back to their lives. I felt as if I were no longer tethered to anything, just moving with the wind. I was beginning to understand the grief Ron felt when he sat alone for months, not moving off the couch or knowing what to do.

Today, three years later, I'm still alone, still grieving. I may not sob as much as I used to, but the emptiness remains. The love is there, but there is no place for it to go. It is emptier, and it's lonelier. I cannot look forward more than a month or two, and I'm still floating with the wind. I am just going through the motions of living with no direction or purpose. But I'm still trying to move, to find my purpose again and embrace simple pleasures. That is this widow's grief. And my widow's code of conduct is to keep pushing through the days until I find that I can believe in my sense of self and purpose again.

# 19

## Is It Fear and Sorrow or Sorrow and Fear?

We are often defined by seminal moments in our lives, but we seldom realize the extent to which they define us. Are we driven by fear or by sorrow? Or is it something else entirely? And how does that affect our emotional health and professional successes? I find myself asking these questions in my late sixties and wondering why I never delved more into my emotional reactions before this age.

Our professional lives are defined by both our successes and our failures, but our emotional security or maturity is so different. I'm just beginning to realize how much of who I became was determined by the early trauma of my mother's illness and subsequent death. I have always known these events helped to determine my view of life's circumstances, but I never realized specifically how. And I never had the courage to explore it in depth before now. I did know that every time I mentioned my mother's death, I would tear up and my voice would crack. Sorrow for the past or fear of the future? These are the things I think about after Ron's death. There are so many questions every day I ask myself.

To attempt to answer these questions, I had to go back to my childhood. As a young girl, I wasn't told much about important things happening around me and to me, because of my mother's illness. I knew my mother was sick, but I didn't understand how sick. I can only remember visiting her in the hospital once over a couple years. I remember only a few times when she was home from the hospital. Since I don't remember anyone talking to me about her illness, I had to rely on my emotional intuitiveness and my eavesdropping, which entailed sitting on the stairway landing and trying to hear what the adults were talking about, even though I had no idea what they were talking about. I don't know if talking to me more about what was happening would have helped or not. I do know that not talking to me left me a very anxious child and therefore an anxious adult. This is where the question of fear or sorrow comes into play.

Ron was also an anxious child for different reasons. He was traumatized by his mother nearly smothering him. I was traumatized by my mother's illness and death. I find it incredible we found each other and could help soothe each other and give each other the necessary courage to overcome that anxiety and to have the courage to excel in our lives together.

I find it puzzling why our most anxious moments were not related to professional achievements or goals. Each of us at times lived high-profile lives in our work; we were often reported on in *The Washington Post*. Somehow, we were able to put on a shield and head into the "battle" of politics without fear, but it just didn't work when it came to our emotional selves.

As time passed, my psychologist told me I seemed calmer, and he asked me why I thought that might be. I told him I no longer had to worry every day about Ron. In the last few years of Ron's life, I worried constantly if I was away from home traveling for more than a day. At the end, I couldn't leave the house for even a few hours without hiring a caregiver. I worried that I would have to place him in an assisted-living facility, and I had no idea how I could do that emotionally and financially. Ron had consented to enter a nursing home for twenty-six days leading up to his surgery to address his bladder issues and prevent further urinary tract infections. It was horrible for both of us, so I knew if I had to do that on a permanent basis, it would be unbearable. But now, he is no longer in emotional distress or physical pain.

I managed to survive Ron's death, and I wasn't always sure I would. I managed to write Ron's obituary and organize the celebration of his life. I managed to establish a fully endowed memorial scholarship in his name at the University of Oklahoma, funded by donations from his friends. But dealing with daily life remained a challenge for a very long time. I knew I needed to begin to visualize the future. I also knew Ron would not want me to be frozen like he was. I knew I needed to start building my future without him, but how would I do that?

After Ron's death I rarely dreamed. But one night I dreamed Ron and I and my parents were inside a new house, deciding whether to purchase it. For some reason, I had to go back to our current house and leave my parents there until I returned. When it was time for me to go back to meet them, I needed to ride my bike to get there. This bike in my dream had very big tires, and the seat was very high. I remember thinking in my dream I couldn't get up on the seat or even reach the pedals for fear of falling. Somehow, I jumped up on the bike and began to pedal. Not only was I high above the ground, but I had to ride down a very steep mountainside full of big rocks. I was afraid I would fall off the side of the mountain, but I kept pedaling as if my life depended on it. I never got to that new house, but I kept pedaling, and not once did I falter or fall. I woke up after that dream with a different feeling. For the first time in quite a while, I thought maybe my brain was telling me I could do it on my own; it wouldn't be easy, but I could believe in myself again.

# 20

---

# Decision-Making
## *The Big Move*

There were a few things I needed to do to start my life again without my partner. The biggest and most important thing was to move. I liked Leesburg, but I had never liked our home there. So, I called a friend who was a realtor, and we began the hunt in earnest. A few months after my search began and after several promising home visits and failed offers, I saw a house on the internet that was promising. It was situated on three acres in a town ten miles from my current location. I had no idea what the inside was like, but the fact that it had acreage and a pond promised a peaceful place where I thought I might be able to heal. On Friday, February 10, the first day the house was being shown, my realtor and I scheduled a morning appointment. The photos of the house had been posted the evening before, so I had some idea of the inside.

When I drove up the driveway, with a pond and geese on my right, up to the top of the hill where the home was,

I thought this could be the place. I wasn't scared or anxious, just ready. We walked inside, and I knew this was it. It was calm and cozy and welcoming: just what I liked. Many potential buyers were in and out of the house, so I assumed the owners would be getting numerous offers by Friday afternoon. We were the first to send in an offer. We built into the offer an escalation clause for the purchase price and decided to forego a home inspection as an added incentive. I was hopeful, but I had viewed several properties before seeing this one, made offers, and none had been accepted, so I didn't let myself get too excited.

We heard nothing about our offer over the weekend, and by Monday evening I had convinced myself that once again I was stuck in this house that I felt desperate to leave. No sooner had I resigned myself to being stuck when my realtor called and said, "They accepted our offer!" She was almost as excited as I was. This is the realtor who had helped Ron and me sell our long-standing home just a few years before, when I had been a basket case. Now, for the first time in a long time, I began to feel a little bit of hope for my future.

Three days later, I was on a plane to Venice, Italy, by myself, to celebrate my birthday. For many years before this, Ron and I had flown to Florida to celebrate my birthday on the beach. Since my birthday falls between Valentine's Day and the President's Day congressional recess, it made for a nice break in the winter. But I wanted to break out of the mold, so I decided to make the very bold move of celebrating Carnivale in Venice.

I landed in Venice on my sixty-eighth birthday. I was alone, but it was okay. I had researched all the travel books, scheduled a few tours and classes through my travel agent, and I was as ready as I was going to be. I took a tourist gondola from my hotel on the Grand Canal and began to make my way through the narrow streets and over the many bridges to find the location where I was to meet my private gondola. I was fascinated by all the people dressed in period clothing and masks for Carnivale, like being in a fairy tale and traveling through time.

I had booked a one-hour private gondola ride under the Bridge of Sighs and through the many waterways, accompanied by the gondolier and two musicians, a guitarist and a singer. This was my birthday present to me! The singer sang several famous Italian songs, and I sang along to the ones I knew. When he sang "Que Será Será" the first tear fell—that was something Ron would say, not sing thankfully, "Whatever will be, will be." When the singer on the gondola began singing Happy Birthday—not only in English but Italian—the tears really began to flow. But I wasn't particularly sad. I felt nostalgic for my old life but also hopeful for my new one. It was so perfect and comforting that I felt I could have been wrapped in Ron's arms.

Before I left on my trip, I had found a Facebook group "Solo in Style: Women Over 50 Travelling Solo and Loving It!" Who knew there were so many women my age who were traveling solo! I had a great time reading about their many adventures and their stories from all around the world.

One of the posts came from a group called "Venice/Girl Gone International." I was accepted into their group and was thrilled to see they organized weekly "Spritz Time" gatherings—there was one scheduled for my birthday night in Venice. This was just too much of a coincidence to not go and meet these women, learn where they were all from, and enjoy an Aperol spritz, a drink I had never had. A mix of prosecco, Aperol, soda water, and an orange slice, it has quickly become my favorite drink.

There were six of us, all single, who met: one Venetian, four Americans, and one Canadian. We met at a local bar for drinks and *cicchetti* (Italian for small bites) and had such a great time we moved to another restaurant and wine bar for my first meal in Venice. We shared our life stories and told what had brought us to Venice. It was a perfect way to spend my first birthday without Ron.

Gioia, one of the Venetian women in the group, helped me navigate my way back to the hotel along the narrow, empty streets and alleyways that seemed to be a maze. She explained that Venice is a very safe city, and a woman walking alone at night should have no problem. By the time I reached my hotel, it was after 11 p.m. Since I'd traveled over-night the night before and was operating on very little sleep, I was more than ready to hit the bed. I looked back on the day, my birthday, and I was content—maybe not happy, but at least content. It was a beginning. I slept a peaceful, exhausted, and satisfied sleep that night.

My eyes popped open at 6 a.m. ready for a full day of planned activities. I confidently hopped a water taxi (I was starting to learn how to navigate Venice) and found my way to the Murano glass artist studio, where, after a lesson, I made my own glass pendant. I then made my way to my scheduled mask-making class. It was Carnivale after all, and everyone needed a mask.

What fun I had picking a mask, deciding on colors, and painting it. Making things for me usually means I'm only thinking about what my hands are making, and that was a good thing. For the months leading up to this, I couldn't focus on much of anything, nor did I have the desire. I had no capacity for creativity. I wasn't ready yet to let my mind focus. Everywhere I looked, people in costumes were smiling and having a good time. The joy was beginning to feel contagious. I made my way to the oldest coffee shop in Venice, Caffè Florian on the square, where I would meet my guide for the day's tour.

We toured all the usual tourist sites as my guide Alvise explained the history of the Doge's Palace; how the Bridge of Sighs got its name; Acqua Alta, the famous bookstore where there were so many books they were even used as steps; and the Rialto Bridge with all the shops. Like any good tour guide, he was friendly with several local artisan shops where I bought a pair of handcrafted dog earrings. We walked over eight miles that day, and I learned a lot about Venice and maybe about myself.

The day concluded in what I thought the most appropriate way: seated in my front-row seat in Vivaldi's church with his "Four Seasons" concert performed by four violinists, a pianist, and two cellists. It was the most incredibly uplifting experience I think I could have experienced at that moment. The music was light and hopeful and made me feel fresh and alive. It made me feel like spring instead of winter. Maybe being in Venice at Carnivale at the time of Lent was my metaphor about rebirth in a sense. For the first time in a long time, I wasn't running somewhere, or as my granddaughter would say I was not on a mission for anyone or anything. I was taking time to absorb Venice. It was a strange feeling to do just that and only that. And it was a marvelous day.

On my final full day in Venice, I arranged for a tour of the neighboring islands of Murano and Burano. A quick thirty-minute boat ride and we were inside a glass-blowing factory on Murano. Then we went by boat to Burano and watched how the famous lace is crafted still today. That night in Venice, I attended the opera at Scuola Grande San Teodoro. Since the Italians essentially invented opera, when you're in Italy, you must go to the opera!

I was tired and ready to go home the next day, but was so glad I had made the leap and taken the trip alone. I had considered asking my sister or another family member to go with me, since I was already paying for the hotel room, but I am glad I did not. I learned I can have a wonderful time entertaining myself. I liked doing what I wanted when I wanted, and I loved exploring.

# 21

---

# Making the Big Move

The first few weeks after the move to my new home felt much like the get-out-the-vote efforts at the end of a campaign. I remembered the feeling I had during the Senate race of 1994: it was intense, it was exhausting, and it was exhilarating, all at the same time. That was much of what I was feeling now, moving to my new home. I was hopeful I could build a new life, but my energy tank was running low. Despite that, I got up every morning before dawn and kept moving until I collapsed in the evening: up and down the stairs, up and down the stairs again, emptying boxes, moving furniture, and hanging pictures. Ron never felt he was home until pictures were hung on the wall, and I had the same feeling. The boxes seemed never-ending, and they were filled with memories.

I woke up every morning, looked outside my window, and felt grateful, if not more at peace. Everywhere I looked on my three acres I saw green grass, trees, deer, a pond and geese, and space—loads of it. This house reminded me of the home we owned in Great Falls: it was quiet and peaceful; it wasn't fussy; it was rustic. It wasn't in the city; it was in the country. It was more me and what I needed now. Ron would love to say he liked to feel the concrete between his toes, funny for a boy from rural Oklahoma. But I preferred the grass and the calm I felt surrounded by nature. And the dogs loved it even more than I did. They ran and chased each other while I watched and enjoyed it along with them.

Finally, on a Saturday a few weeks in, I just could not move anymore. I told myself I had to rest; no point in having a heart attack now. So, with a blanket in hand, I plopped myself on the couch and prepared for an afternoon of television binge-watching, surrounded by my dogs.

There are many unexplained events where I felt Ron was sending me a message—a message of love and encouragement. I have no idea about these things, but in the past, I have felt the presence of my mother or father, so now I tend to pay attention and be open to those feelings. If that makes me a little nutty, so be it.

I found, as I watched a television show about a widow, that there were many times I said out loud to the television, "I did that!" As I watched one of the last episodes of the season, the main character was pictured alone in her apartment window, sitting in front of her computer, writing about her life and grief after losing her husband. Well, that's what I had been doing too! And, as in the episode entitled "And Just Like That," I decided it was time to continue to write. I had taken three months away from writing, but maybe it was time to start again, this time about my campaign to live life again.

I also decided it was time to get off antidepressants, not particularly a wise decision without talking to my doctor, but I had taken them for too long and simply wanted to be free of them. I was beginning to feel stronger and thought this was something I could do. (I do not encourage anyone to make this decision!) There were times, as I weaned myself off them, I felt I would jump out of my skin.

I now found that writing calmed me—a completely new experience for me. Writing had always been a "chore" for me, but now it was an outlet. I asked my psychologist what he thought about this. He said he didn't know for sure, but the reason therapy works is you must put words and sentences to your thoughts and feelings to make sense of them. I had a lifetime of thoughts and feelings that needed to be expressed, in words, out loud. I had so much more to express than I had ever thought. Until this time I had followed my father's and husband's examples in just putting feelings in a box in your head and moving forward. While I talked a lot, I never really expressed how I felt during those tough times, so now was as good a time as any. And probably long overdue.

## 22

---

# Widow's Code of Conduct?

The first year of my life as a widow was hell. I had to live through all the firsts—birthdays, anniversaries, Thanksgiving, Christmas, New Year's, election days, and more. I thought I was ready to emerge from my grief, but I felt completely vulnerable. And alone. I hadn't felt vulnerable when I managed my first statewide campaign with all the odds against us and managed to be awarded a Pollie Award for campaign manager of the year by my peers. I hadn't felt vulnerable when then Senator Joe Biden chose me to be his chief of staff on Capitol Hill. And I hadn't felt an ounce of vulnerability when I entered the Democratic primary for lieutenant governor of Virginia. Hell, even my own radio show didn't faze me. But the feeling of emotional vulnerability following Ron's death was completely debilitating.

Right after Ron's death, friends and family encircled me with warmth and sympathy, and I was deeply grateful for that support. But then people moved on with their own lives and families, as they should have and needed to do. Yet, I was still in that place of darkness. I didn't want to be a burden to my friends, so I mostly said I was fine when someone asked. Inside, I was far from fine.

By long tradition, one year is the socially accepted amount of time for mourning the loss of a spouse. I found, however, there was nothing I could do to hurry the process along, as much as I would try. Still, as the one-year mark approached, I felt the need to find a new purpose. When I was a campaign manager, the purpose was clear: help my candidate win. The goal was also clear: my work ended once the election was held. But in this situation, there was no election day, and I couldn't figure out how to organize and plan this campaign. There were no votes to count, no groups to organize, and the only persuasion to be done was inside my own head.

Having spent the past year alone or with other female friends, and thankful for them, I was very much in need of expanding that circle again. Given how I had spent my professional life, I missed the normal interactions with men: sharing a laugh, telling a funny story, or discussing something of interest. But now I felt uncomfortable when I talked with men, as if I was behaving inappropriately.

The relationship with couples who were Ron's and my friends also changed. I was no longer one half of a couple, and many of my friends expected that I would only want to spend time with the other women.

I did new things during that first year: I got a new puppy, bringing the total number of dogs to four. I organized the celebration of life at Ron's favorite Capitol Hill watering hole. I created a memorial scholarship in Ron's name at his alma mater. I went on weekend trips with girlfriends. I tried to work—not well—but enough. It was difficult to focus, but I kept trying. I took a trip to Europe; I bought a new house and sold my old one. But there were weeks when I barely moved. Any project to fight off my loneliness? I tried it. Sometimes it worked; many times it failed. I didn't say no to anything.

After Ron's death, my sense of self was forever changed. I was no longer the same person: I didn't laugh as freely as before, I didn't look into the future, and the small things that would've sent me over the edge before no longer seemed important. I desperately wanted to again embrace all life had to offer before. I wanted to go back to being adventurous, purposeful, bold, daring, and hopeful. So, if there is a widow's code of conduct, it should include understanding and patience with yourself, and forbearance as you learn to navigate the grieving process. I know life gets better, and I'm thankful to those that surround me for that understanding and compassion.

# 23

---

# Boots on the Fence

As the first anniversary of Ron's death grew closer, I decided I needed to have a party. I wanted to make new memories with friends in my new home. I wanted to fill my house with laughter and music.

I designed an invitation with Ron's signature cowboy boots and hat and an American flag for Flag Day. I planned to have live country music from a local band benefiting a music charity founded by a friend, and food and drinks promoting local restaurants and vineyards. While this was the one-year anniversary of Ron's passing, I did not want it to be about that. I needed to begin the next chapter in my life—with Ron in my heart instead of by my side. I sent invitations to longtime friends and new ones—people Ron and I enjoyed, neighbors and politicians.

A week before the party, I experienced a major downward trajectory in my mood. I cried constantly and felt frozen in place. I regretted planning a party and had no idea how I would survive it. What the hell was I thinking planning a function with fifty people on the day before the one-year anniversary of losing Ron? It was just too much, and I doubted whether I could hold it together emotionally. Then my nephew texted me that he and his wife were coming from Virginia Beach, and I felt a little bit of hope. I knew my nephew looked up to me, and I didn't want him to see me in my current emotional state; his text was just what I needed to gather myself and buck up.

The day of the party arrived, and everything was ready—but was I? The dogs must have felt something exciting was going to happen; they were up and jumping on the bed at four thirty in the morning. Reluctantly and sleepily, I got up. I was on autopilot, trying not to think too much, just getting everything ready for the afternoon party. My nephew and his wife arrived to help me set things up, and I started to feel a little better. I loved having them around.

It was going to be a sunny, warm summer day, great for an afternoon outdoor gathering. When people began to arrive, I felt a slight shift in my mood. I wasn't alone. I was happy to see friends coming to my new place to make new happy memories. People were smiling and laughing, having a fun time, and so was I. I fell into bed that night exhausted, but feeling lighter, even a little happy.

When I awoke the next morning, the first thought I had was, *Today is the day*: the one-year anniversary of losing Ron. I had planned to spend the day alone, with my thoughts, but there was one thing I needed to do.

Ron had enough pairs of cowboy boots to wear a different pair every day of the week. They were alligator skins, ostrich skins, lizard skins, and more. They were black, brown, and cordovan. And they were all in perfect, well-maintained condition. Every Sunday night, Ron cleaned, treated, and polished all seven pairs of boots.

When he died, I tried to give his treasured boots to the male members of our family, but none of them wore his shoe size. I couldn't donate them, along with his other clothes, to Goodwill, so I hung on to them.

One day an article popped up on my computer with the headline "If You See a Boot on a Fence, This Is What It Means." The article said a cowboy boot on a fence post has special meaning. It means the person's work is done. It honors the person who wore them for a life well-lived. The article also said that one must always hang them bottoms up so the soul of the cowboy could go to heaven. I knew what I had to do.

That morning, I chose a pair of Ron's boots and placed them on opposite sides on the new fence post on my property. It was a good and traditional way to honor Ron and his life of purpose. It felt right, and I was satisfied. It marked the end of the chapter of our lives together as well as marking the start of the next chapter of my life.

Many years ago, I had bought T-shirts for Ron and me that said, "Do scary things that don't kill you," and we lived out that saying: we lived boldly, at times with abandon, and we surprised ourselves.

By some standards, our lives weren't extraordinary. The choices we made with a leap of faith, the chances we took, and the opportunities we created made them extraordinary for us. Now I was learning how to do scary things that didn't kill me—alone.

# 24

# Learning to Embrace the Memory of Love

My campaign to find a way forward with my new reality progressed. There were days when the fog of grief would clear, and I would remember the feeling of looking forward to things again. On other days, I felt like I was superglued to my chair. There were enough of those days that I gained almost twenty pounds, so I made a commitment to move my body,

I began walking a mile and a half every day on my hilly gravel country road. It's good aerobic exercise, and the sights and smells of nature gave me comfort: does with their fawns, hawks, geese, an occasional fox or wild turkey. Often, I pretended to see Ron smiling and waving at me.

One weekend, I talked myself into going to an exhibit of Native American art at the Renwick Gallery in DC. The show focused on two themes: the burdens you carry and those you wish to honor. One artist's work honored her deceased parent, who died during the COVID-19 pandemic. The exhibit consisted of three raw leather "body bags" beaded at the top with a pattern of colors. Another was a blanket of beads with the patterns of the DNA of an illness draped over several wolf statues. Honors and Burdens.

I treated myself to lunch, then went window shopping. While walking, I played with my wedding ring, which I often did. Suddenly, it came off my finger. I stopped and stood there, looking at my naked finger, feeling the enormity of what had just happened.

I know that I will always love and miss Ron. I don't know why I removed my ring that day; I didn't feel any less married. I put the ring back on several weeks later and continue to wear it.

The next day, I went for my usual walk but continued walking farther, to Lincoln, the little local village founded by Quakers during the Civil War. As I approached the Quaker meetinghouse, I was greeted by a very welcoming woman who invited me inside. She described their Sunday services where they would sit silently facing each other in contemplation until, or if, someone had something they wanted to share. I did not participate that day, but I was interested and thought I might want to revisit them sometime. On the way home, I stopped at my neighbor's B&B at the end of my road. She has chickens and ducks and sells freshly picked blueberries and eggs. She's quite a bit older than me and has been a widow for many years. While we talked on her porch, my emotions started to rise to the surface. She told me, "Susan, it takes three years to recover from your husband's death; don't ask too much of yourself."

One morning, I looked in the mirror and thought, *Hello, I think I recognize you.* For the year leading up to Ron's death and the year following, I didn't feel like myself, nor did I recognize myself. My mind wandered. I couldn't focus, and about the only things I could manage to do were the daily rituals—brush my teeth, feed the dogs, and do it all over again the next day. Gradually, I began to recognize myself again in the mirror. Was I coming back?

No campaign is a straight path to victory. There are now moments when I can think of my life and smile.

# 25
---
# My New Season of Giving

I love giving gifts. I like to think about just the right gifts for family and friends throughout the year. Sometimes the gifts are small and fun, and sometimes they are extraordinary. Sometimes I make the gifts, and sometimes I cook them, and once I even gave a four-legged new best friend. It has always given me immense joy to give gifts to those I care about and who were kind to me during the year.

In my first season of giving without Ron, I found myself completely alone. The remaining members of my extended family had formed new traditions that didn't include me. I needed to create new traditions of my own.

In November, I gave a "Cassoulet in the Country" dinner party with a dozen women friends with whom I had exercised and traveled with for more than fifteen years. The dinner turned out to be a gift to me more fulfilling than I could have imagined. I created little touches to add to the hygge feeling I wanted to create. I had sparkly lights and shiny angel wings around the table. I chose quotes to put at each place setting that I thought would be appropriate for each woman. The fire was blazing in the fireplace, and my screened porch was joyous with fairy lights and decorations even hanging from the ceiling. One of my friends created a special candy cane cocktail, and others brought salads and dessert. After dinner, we moved to the living room to exchange gifts. We opened candles, chocolate, socks, and bath oils—and we laughed. I had not felt more comforted, fulfilled, and warm in a long time.

But I still had to face Christmas dinner on my own. One dear friend asked what I was doing for Christmas Day. When I said I had no plans, she said she would come over with her daughter. I was more than thrilled. She knew I liked to cook, and we enjoyed each other's comfortable company. Then my neighbor posted on social media she was looking for a restaurant open on Christmas for her and her eighty-five-year-old father, as her husband was going to be out of town. So, I asked them to join us too.

So, gift-giving was different this year, but it turned out to be quite wonderful.

# 26

---

# The Changing
# Adventures on the Wall

When Ron and I were involved in politics, we had a brag wall consisting of photos of the two of us shaking hands or otherwise engaging with a governor, senator, congressman, and even the president. Most were signed by that person with "to my good friend." Now, my brag wall is changing.

Almost one year after my trip to Venice, I read an article on social media about a place inside the Arctic Circle—Tromso, Norway—that was celebrating National Sami Week. The Sami people are reindeer herders who survive in the frigid weather inside the Arctic Circle. Like my visit to Venice to celebrate Carnivale, I was pulled to this new adventure. I had gone an entire year not even considering traveling alone again, and then this possibility came along and ignited a spark.

I dismissed the temptation to live with the Sami for four days during the herding of reindeer—there were no bathroom facilities or showers. Instead, I planned activities that started in a heated minivan outside my hotel in Tromso.

The timing of my trip coincided with good weather for travel. The week before, Norway had experienced a once-in-a-hundred-years weather event where roofs were blown off, schools and businesses were closed, and all tours cancelled. The government warned people not to leave their homes. And I thought zero temperatures were bad enough! But the Norwegians never complain about the weather. They say there is no such thing as bad weather, only bad clothing, but that week all bets were off.

When I arrived in Tromso, it was a balmy eighteen degrees Celsius (about sixty-five degrees). I have always said I would rather be cold than hot, and this trip was going to test that theory, but I was prepared. I had wool long underwear, fleece tights, and puffy overpants. I had wool sweaters, two pairs of gloves and mittens, a new, long Helly Hansen overcoat, Canadian boots, and an Iceland sherpa hat, not to mention spikes for my boots.

I checked into my hotel and discovered it was also the home base for most of my tours. The view from the windows of my room was something out of a travel magazine: fjords and waterfront, fishing ships and saunas, the Arctic Chapel and a cable car to the top of the mountain. It seemed appropriate that the "Troll Museum" and folklore stories were right next door!

Each day was another amazing adventure that topped the one of the day before. The first experience was reindeer sledding and feeding, followed by storytelling by an authentic Sami reindeer herder inside a fireplace-warmed yurt and eating reindeer stew. A moonlight sled ride included a green slice of northern lights.

Early the next morning, I met the bus that would drive us to Finland for snowmobiling. We left the hotel at 6:30 a.m., so we were in darkness until about 10 a.m. It was just two weeks from the end of polar nights on January 21, when the hours of daylight increased daily until the night was almost banished—the time of the midnight sun.

Ron and I had once gone snowmobiling in winter in Yellowstone Park, but he drove, and I just held on. This time I was going solo for three hours, traveling to the place where Finland's, Norway's, and Sweden's borders met. With my four layers of clothing and reindeer fur insoles in my boots, I was plenty warm, even though I felt like the Michelin man. I traveled the twelve miles of snow path to the marker in minus twenty-five-degree weather. I was proud of myself, and the view was magnificent. Ron would have been as proud of me as well, and I wished he was beside me to talk about the marvelous and challenging day.

The last item on my bucket list for this trip was witnessing the aurora borealis, or northern lights. Ten years earlier, on a trip to Iceland, I had seen a little bit of purple in the sky, but since Tromso is supposed to be the best place on earth to witness the lights, I was counting on witnessing them in their full glory. Outside Tromso, we traveled to a family farm owned by a chef who served farm-to-table food she had grown. She embraced me because I was wearing a Sami hat I had bought the day before, and after dinner she tried to teach me how to sing Sami. Our guide ran into the yurt to tell us the northern lights were appearing. We all rushed out to witness the fantastic green and purple lights dancing across the sky. The night was magic.

I still had one day in Tromso to shop at the Sami market— I could not leave without reindeer antlers and skin from the Sami herder. I was in awe of what I experienced on this trip. I felt very much alive and looked forward to the next day's events.

After I returned home and recovered from jet lag, I found myself again looking at my brag wall of adventures in my office. Until now, I could not envision adding to those pictures—nothing lived up to those trips with Ron. But now, I thought I might add photos I had taken of reindeer sledding, northern lights hunting, and snowmobiling. Alongside a photo of Ron and me dog sledding in Canada, I put the photo of me in the reindeer's sled, pulled by Vellya. Across from the photo of Ron and me tandem parasailing, I put the photo of me with the northern lights above my head. A photo of me on the snowmobile was added to one with Ron and me together on a snowmobile. I even added the photo of me in the gondola with a mask from the trip to Venice the year before. It was a start.

# 27

---

# Fake It till You Make It

Charles Darwin said, "It is not the most intelligent of the species that survives; it is not the strongest that survives; but the species that survives is the one that is able best to adapt and adjust to the changing environment in which it finds itself."[3]

I still have not adapted well to life as a widow, but I continue to work on it. I am still a bit untethered, but I'm trying to ground myself. I am still lonely, but I'm getting used to it. I'm not ashamed to admit that, at my doctor's advice, I now take a double dose of antidepressants, and sometimes need to add a Xanax to that. When I feel like I'm about to fall into the abyss, I call my psychologist, and he tells me not to expect too much of myself. I can even say now that I am enjoying my alone time in my new home in the country with all the animals, and I'm learning more about who I am now.

I don't know where I thought I would be emotionally at this point, but it doesn't really matter. I'm learning to accept where and who I am now. I plan for travel or to entertain just to encourage myself. I'm not sure I will ever fall in love again and am not sure I would want to. One or another of the dogs sleeps in the bed with me on Ron's side, under a blanket of Ron's old T-shirts sewn together. Those puppies continue to give me reasons to get up in the morning, and they do make me laugh. Ron's toothbrush is still in its holder in the bathroom, and I still wear his Oklahoma T-shirt to bed. There are still times, when I'm doing something that's interesting, I think *I have to call Ron*, and then I remember again that I can't.

My sister, Jessica, and I have taken weekend trips to New York City to take in a few Broadway shows. On Easter weekend, we went to see the new Broadway musical about the suffragists' fight for the vote and the Equal Rights Amendment, and the next day we joined in the fun in the Easter Parade down Fifth Avenue.

Jessica said no to wearing a hat in the parade, but I got a fascinator that had two birds flying above a nest with an egg inside. I had a great time wearing that crazy hat and walking down Fifth Avenue enjoying everyone's else's creative and outrageous hats. We laughed and took pictures of ourselves and other people enjoying a beautiful spring day in New York City. The next day, after we arrived back home, Jessica sent me a text with a picture from one hundred years ago of a woman wearing a hat that was a chicken with a full complement of feathers and a bow tied around its neck, its beak held high. The caption read, "Some days you just add a bow tie to your chicken hat and get on with life the best you can." Jessica wrote, "This is something you would say."

Two important thoughts occurred to me following that weekend. The first was the message of the play: keep fighting and keep marching. The second important thought of the weekend came from Jessica's note, when I realized that was what I had determined to do: dress up and get on with life the best I could—with an imaginary chicken on my head. I realized I do not have to continue with the same urgency of purpose that I had throughout my life. It is time to look to my granddaughter Kristin, who has taken up the fight for women's justice and healthcare. It's her turn, but I can help and encourage her along the way because of what I have lived and experienced.

Like me, Kristin lost her mother, my stepdaughter Karen, when she was young, so she and her brother spent quite a bit of time with Ron and me. I remember one time when she was visiting, she heard me telling Ron I needed my flat tire fixed. Kristin turned to me and said in a sarcastic way that only a teenager can, "But SuSu, as a feminist you should fix the tire for yourself."

Not sure how to respond because I really didn't want to change the tire but did want to say something about being a feminist, I replied, "Being a feminist means I get to choose for myself, and I choose not to fix that tire." I guess some lessons got through, because now she has begun organizing and speaking on behalf of women and their rights. I am enormously proud of her.

Writing this memoir was the hardest thing I have ever done. Many times, I wished that Ron were with me to help me remember and correct me or edit my words. It would have made the writing a whole lot easier, but then the story would not be complete. In politics, it's important to tell a good story, but I have lived it and it's been a great one. What more can you ask for in one life, besides that and a good pair of cowboy boots?

# RECIPES

## Fried Steak and Pan Gravy

This dish is the unofficial state dish of Texas and migrated up to Oklahoma. There are many different varieties of this recipe, but this version was one of Ron's favorites. **Note:** Not calorie friendly!

### INGREDIENTS

Beef bottom round or similar cuts of beef
Flour
Salt and pepper to taste
Beaten eggs
Vegetable oil
Unsalted chicken broth
Milk

### DIRECTIONS

Cut meat against the grain in half-inch thick slices. Dredge steak in flour mixed with salt and pepper. Tenderize meat with mallet or needling device until meat is very thin. Repeat dredging in flour and beaten egg twice. Heat vegetable oil in skillet, and when it is hot, add meat. Cook on both sides until brown, 3 or 4 minutes. Set on wire rack. Add a few more tablespoons of vegetable oil to pan. Whisk a few more tablespoons of flour with the oil and cook until gravy begins to simmer. Add chicken broth and whisk until combined and gravy thickens. Add milk and continue whisking until gravy falls off spoon. Serve gravy over steaks.

# Haluski (Cabbage and Noodles)

With the many central and eastern Europeans settling in the Pittsburgh area, there are just as many recipes for haluski as there are noodles. This simple and economical dish, now made with store-bought noodles, was a favorite of mine.

### INGREDIENTS

2 T. butter
1 yellow onion
Salt and pepper to taste
1 head green cabbage
1 12-ounce package wide egg noodles

### DIRECTIONS

Melt butter, then add onion with salt and pepper and cook until lightly browned. Thinly slice the cabbage and combine with onion, adding more salt and pepper to taste, stirring until cabbage is tender but not mushy (20–30 minutes). Meanwhile, cook noodles per package instructions in boiling water. Reserve a half cup pasta water and drain noodles. Add cooked noodles, reserved pasta water, and remaining butter to cabbage and onion. Stir for a few minutes over medium heat until noodles are saucy. Season with more salt and pepper.

# ENDNOTES

1   Ted Kennedy, "1980 Democratic National Concession Address," American Rhetoric, August 12, 1980, https://www.americanrhetoric.com/speeches /tedkennedy1980dnc.htm.

2   Reba McEntire, "3 'Bones' You Must Have," Oprah's Master Class, Oprah Winfrey Network, YouTube, March 5, 2012, 1:08, https://www.youtube.com/watch ?v=XQCrSI_hhkA.

3   "Darwin Correspondence Project," University of Cambridge, accessed October 16, 2024, https://www .darwinproject.ac.uk/people/about-darwin/six-things -darwin-never-said/evolution-misquotation.

# ACKNOWLEDGMENTS

Authoring a book of any kind is an enormous task. I found writing this book about my life with the man of my dreams to be tortuous at times, heart-wrenching at times, funny, and by the end, quite fulfilling. I am not a writer by nature, but life compelled me this time. In sharing my story of overcoming loss, fighting direction, great love, and purpose, I have learned a lot about myself as I reflect on those who have shared in my life and helped me in so many ways along the way.

First and foremost, my husband of forty-three years, Ron Platt, who made my life—and ours together—quite an adventure. He made my life more magical than I could ever have imagined or hoped for, and I miss him every day.

To my mother, Julia Gaslevic Smocer, who knew she would not live long enough to see the person I would become but made sure she laid a path of leadership in her life for me to follow. My rock for sixty years was my father, Anthony Vincent Smocer. His commonsense advice, steadiness, kindness, and perseverance were fitting examples of how to navigate a fulfilling life after the loss of his wife. And for Barbara LaRosa Smocer, my stepmother, who became my mother and friend. She never treated me any differently than her birth children and showed me great love and understanding.

My gratitude goes out to all the members of the Smocer family, and Ron's son, Keith, and his wife, Luisa. To all our grandchildren, but particularly our granddaughter Kristin, who has shown great resilience after her mother's struggles. I cannot wait to see all she accomplishes. It has been a joy to watch her grow to become such a strong, smart, and fun woman and now mother of two girls who will eventually become president. She has been a wonderful support system for me.

Politics is a tough business, and I want to thank Senator Chuck Robb and Lynda Johnson Robb for putting their faith in me to lead the 1994 senate reelection campaign. President Joe Biden hired me to be his chief of staff in the Senate at a time of change on the Hill. He was a tremendous example of perseverance and picking yourself up after great tragedy. I think about that often in my new role as a widow. I learned so much about politics and myself while working for these elected political leaders. Thank yous go to all my fellow Democratic political friends, leaders, and campaign workers throughout Virginia and across the country, who have enriched my life and helped provide loads of laughs and remarkable stories to tell from the campaign trail.

I tip my hat to all the women who gathered in Critz, Virginia, in 2008 when collectively we formed the first Democratic statewide organization dedicated to electing more women. The twenty-three were led by our host and inspiration, former Virginia Attorney General Mary Sue Terry. We have elected many smart women to political office, and we are not even close to how much more we can accomplish.

A big hug goes out to my longtime exercise buddies. They rallied around me when I needed it most. They include Myriam Kane, Laura Hamilton, Tina Jay, Gail Romansky, Lori Fisher, Sandy Morris, Michele Leader, and most especially Cathy McDonough and her silly puppy, Watson.

I counted on Neil McNerney's monthly therapy sessions as a time to cry and whine—and then he reminded me that there was more I needed to do, including authoring this book. My friend Ellen Heald got me through the early days with our daily check-in calls at the time I needed it most.

I am most grateful to Jim and Candace Brown of Florence, South Carolina. Their generosity to the Ronald L. Platt Memorial Scholarship for Political Science at the University of Oklahoma has helped ensure another young person from Ada, Oklahoma, can attend college and study our government.

Michele Orwin was the first person to whom I reached out to help me draft this book. I had a story to tell but no idea what I was doing and no faith in my ability to write something anyone would want to read. As my book coach, she encouraged me, laughed at my stories, suggested edits for my writing, and understood the motivation behind it. It was at her instigation I sent my manuscript to Bold Story Press. When I would get flustered and frustrated, she suggested I think about it over an Aperol spritz! I will be forever grateful.

It was such a thrill when Emily Barrosse told me that her company, Bold Story Press, wanted to publish my book. I must still be dreaming. And with the help of Nedah Rose, editor at Bold Story Press, my book became something I will forever be proud of.

And finally, to my fabulous four, four-legged furry family members—Twix, Blue2, Rily Rose, and Strawberry—for giving me a reason to get up every morning and always provide loads of entertainment.

There are three things I would recommend to young women searching for their purpose: never underestimate yourself or be defined by your sex or education, choose your loves wisely, and don't be afraid to do scary things that won't kill you.

# ABOUT THE AUTHOR

Susan Smocer Platt's career in politics spans forty years and includes successfully managing the comeback campaign of a US Senator to serving as chief of staff to a future president to running her own campaign for lieutenant governor. Upon her arrival in Washington, DC, she met Ronald Platt, who would become her husband. For the next forty-three years, they walked the halls of Congress and worked in political campaigns across the country.

After the death of her beloved husband in 2022, she sought the comfort of the country in western Loudoun County, Virginia, along with her four dogs, where she continues work in political and legislative consulting.

# ABOUT
# BOLD STORY PRESS

Bold Story Press is a curated, woman-owned hybrid publishing company with a mission of publishing well-written stories by women. If your book is chosen for publication, our team of expert editors and designers will work with you to publish a professionally edited and designed book. Every woman has a story to tell. If you have written yours and want to explore publishing with Bold Story Press, contact us at https://boldstorypress.com.

The Bold Story Press logo, designed by Grace Arsenault, was inspired by the nom de plume, or pen name, a sad necessity at one time for female authors who wanted to publish. The woman's face hidden in the quill is the profile of Virginia Woolf, who, in addition to being an early feminist writer, founded and ran her own publishing company, Hogarth Press.

Made in the USA
Columbia, SC
04 December 2024

245d4b63-13f9-42ab-9736-4d2922065192R01